Unity 2018 Augmented Projects

Build four immersive and fun AR applications using ARKit, ARCore, and Vuforia

Jesse Glover

BIRMINGHAM - MUMBAI

Unity 2018 Augmented Reality Projects

Commissioning Editor: Kunal Chaudhari
Acquisition Editor: Larissa Pinto
Content Development Editor: Francis Carneiro
Technical Editor: Sachin Sunilkumar
Copy Editor: Safis Editing
Project Coordinator: Sheejal Shah
Proofreader: Safis Editing
Indexer: Aishwarya Gangawane
Graphics: Jason Monteiro
Production Coordinator: Deepika Naik

First published: July 2018

Production reference: 1270718

Published by Packt Publishing Ltd.
Livery Place
35 Livery Street
Birmingham
B3 2PB, UK.

ISBN 978-1-78883-876-4

www.packtpub.com

I would, first and foremost, like to thank Packt Publishing for giving me this wonderful opportunity of writing this book for them.

To my mother, Joy Glover, and eldest sister, Jessica Glover, for always believing in me and telling me to follow my dreams.

To Michael Rex, who encouraged me to never give up and to always work hard. Rest in peace, old man.

To my girlfriend, Summer Wang, for being my loving partner and for making sure that I am always improving my skills and knowledge.

To my mentor and perhaps my most awesome friend, Jason Yarber, for teaching me the C# programming language and always being there to answer any questions I had about programming.

To Luke Durback; without him, I would still be very much confused by mathematics.

To whoever is reading this book. I hope you will learn as much from me as I have from my friends.

– Jesse Glover

`mapt.io`

Mapt is an online digital library that gives you full access to over 5,000 books and videos, as well as industry leading tools to help you plan your personal development and advance your career. For more information, please visit our website.

Why subscribe?

- Spend less time learning and more time coding with practical eBooks and Videos from over 4,000 industry professionals

- Improve your learning with Skill Plans built especially for you

- Get a free eBook or video every month

- Mapt is fully searchable

- Copy and paste, print, and bookmark content

PacktPub.com

Did you know that Packt offers eBook versions of every book published, with PDF and ePub files available? You can upgrade to the eBook version at `www.PacktPub.com` and as a print book customer, you are entitled to a discount on the eBook copy. Get in touch with us at `service@packtpub.com` for more details.

At `www.PacktPub.com`, you can also read a collection of free technical articles, sign up for a range of free newsletters, and receive exclusive discounts and offers on Packt books and eBooks.

Contributors

About the author

Jesse Glover is a self-taught software developer and indie game developer who has worked with multiple game engines and has written many tutorials on the subject of game development over the past 8 years. He maintains a YouTube channel dedicated to game development made easy and writes for Zenva in his spare time to teach the ins and outs of game development with Unity, CryEngine, and Unreal Engine, just to name a few. Jesse has also written *Unity Programming for Human Beings*.

I'd like to express my deepest appreciation and special gratitude to the Packt Editorial team that helped me complete this book, especially Francis Carneiro and Sachin Sunilkumar.

I'd also like to thank Larissa Pinto for giving me this book idea and all the developers and engineers who created the tools utilized in this book. I'd like to thank my reviewers, and my girlfriend, Summer Wang, who pushed me to do my best.

About the reviewers

Neil Alexander is a recent graduate from the University of North Carolina at Charlotte, where he earned a master's in computer science with a specialization in intelligent and interactive systems. As part of his education, he worked on developing several virtual reality demos and data visualization applications. He graduated from the Don Bosco Institute of Technology, and has also worked as a research analyst at an IT publishing firm in Mumbai. He currently works as a data scientist with several blockchain and cryptocurrency start-ups in the Washington D.C. area.

Micheal Lanham is a proven software and tech innovator with 20 years of experience. He has developed a broad range of software applications, including games, graphic, web, desktop, engineering, artificial intelligence, GIS, and machine learning applications for a variety of industries. He was introduced to Unity in 2006 and has been an avid developer, consultant, manager, and author of multiple Unity games, graphic projects, and books since. Micheal lives in Calgary, Canada, with his family.

Packt is searching for authors like you

If you're interested in becoming an author for Packt, please visit `authors.packtpub.com` and apply today. We have worked with thousands of developers and tech professionals, just like you, to help them share their insight with the global tech community. You can make a general application, apply for a specific hot topic that we are recruiting an author for, or submit your own idea.

Table of Contents

Preface

Welcome to *Unity 2018 Augmented Reality Projects*. This book is designed for programmers looking to step out of their comfort zones and take the leap into learning about **Augmented Reality (AR)** and how to create projects within Unity with it. We will focus on Android, iOS, and Windows devices and dive deep into understanding the fundamentals of getting started with this amazing and ever-growing technology.

Who this book is for

This book is for anyone looking to expand their current knowledge of Unity. They should have some experience with C# and Unity and should be willing to expose themselves to a little C++, Java, and Objective-C language code as well.

What this book covers

Chapter 1, *What AR is and How to Get Set Up*, explains the processes of installing various SDKs and packages for enabling AR, and building a Hello World example with AR.

Chapter 2, *GIS Fundamentals - The Power of Mapping*, explores the history of GIS, GIS implications in applications and games, and GIS in education.

Chapter 3, *Censored - Various Sensor Data and Plugins*, looks at how to write plugins for Unity in C#, how to write plugins for Unity in C++, how to write plugins for Unity in Objective-C, and how to write plugins for Unity in Java.

Chapter 4, *The Sound of Flowery Prose*, goes into details of the steps for designing an application, looks at conceptualizing the project, and explores how to create an AR application based on the perception of sound.

Chapter 5, *Picture Puzzle - The AR Experience*, helps you design an educational app, learn to use Vuforia, and develop an educational AR application with Vuforia.

Chapter 6, *Fitness for Fun - Tourism and Random Walking*, teaches about Mapbox, integrating Mapbox into Unity, and building a random walk-to-location app prototype.

Chapter 7, *Snap it! Adding Filters to Pictures*, helps you learn about OpenCV, incorporate OpenCV into Unity, build OpenCV from source, and build a facial detection app prototype with OpenCV.

Chapter 8, *To the HoloLens and Beyond*, gives you an insight into the difference between AR and **Mixed Reality (MR)**, teaches you how to use the Hololens simulator, and gets you to build a basic prototype for MR using the Hololens simulator.

To get the most out of this book

To get the most out of this book, you should have some knowledge of the Unity Editor, UI, and build processes. In addition to this, it is highly advised that you have some skill with C# that is above the beginners' level, as this book does not go into how to write C# code. Lastly, it is suggested that you should have, at the very least, taken a look at other programming languages, such as Swift, Objective-C, C, C++, and Java, and are able to get the gist of what is happening with the code that you will encounter in this book at a glance.

The only requirements are basic knowledge of the Unity Game Engine and C#, as they are the primary focuses of this book.

Download the example code files

You can download the example code files for this book from your account at www.packtpub.com. If you purchased this book elsewhere, you can visit www.packtpub.com/support and register to have the files emailed directly to you.

You can download the code files by following these steps:

1. Log in or register at www.packtpub.com.
2. Select the **SUPPORT** tab.
3. Click on **Code Downloads & Errata**.
4. Enter the name of the book in the **Search** box and follow the onscreen instructions.

Once the file is downloaded, please make sure that you unzip or extract the folder using the latest version of:

- WinRAR/7-Zip for Windows
- Zipeg/iZip/UnRarX for Mac
- 7-Zip/PeaZip for Linux

The code bundle for the book is also hosted on GitHub at `https://github.com/PacktPublishing/Unity-2018-Augmented-Reality-Projects`. In case there's an update to the code, it will be updated on the existing GitHub repository.

We also have other code bundles from our rich catalog of books and videos available at `https://github.com/PacktPublishing/`. Check them out!

Download the color images

We also provide a PDF file that has color images of the screenshots/diagrams used in this book. You can download it here: `https://www.packtpub.com/sites/default/files/downloads/Unity2018AugmentedRealityProjects_ColorImages.pdf`.

Conventions used

There are a number of text conventions used throughout this book.

`CodeInText`: Indicates code words in text, database table names, folder names, filenames, file extensions, pathnames, dummy URLs, user input, and Twitter handles. Here is an example: "Create a brand new Unity Project. I will call mine `Snap`."

A block of code is set as follows:

```
struct Circle
{
Circle(int x, int y, int radius) : X(x), Y(y), Radius(radius) {}
int X, Y, Radius;
};
```

When we wish to draw your attention to a particular part of a code block, the relevant lines or items are set in bold:

```
extern "C" void __declspec(dllexport) __stdcall  Close()
{
_capture.release();
}
```

Bold: Indicates a new term, an important word, or words that you see onscreen. For example, words in menus or dialog boxes appear in the text like this. Here is an example: "Select **System info** from the **Administration** panel."

Warnings or important notes appear like this.

 Tips and tricks appear like this.

Get in touch

Feedback from our readers is always welcome.

General feedback: Email feedback@packtpub.com and mention the book title in the subject of your message. If you have questions about any aspect of this book, please email us at questions@packtpub.com.

Errata: Although we have taken every care to ensure the accuracy of our content, mistakes do happen. If you have found a mistake in this book, we would be grateful if you would report this to us. Please visit www.packtpub.com/submit-errata, selecting your book, clicking on the Errata Submission Form link, and entering the details.

Piracy: If you come across any illegal copies of our works in any form on the Internet, we would be grateful if you would provide us with the location address or website name. Please contact us at copyright@packtpub.com with a link to the material.

If you are interested in becoming an author: If there is a topic that you have expertise in and you are interested in either writing or contributing to a book, please visit authors.packtpub.com.

Reviews

Please leave a review. Once you have read and used this book, why not leave a review on the site that you purchased it from? Potential readers can then see and use your unbiased opinion to make purchase decisions, we at Packt can understand what you think about our products, and our authors can see your feedback on their book. Thank you!

For more information about Packt, please visit packtpub.com.

What AR is and How to Get Set up

This book begins with some introductory information and theory regarding **Augmented Reality (AR)**. Unfortunately, we can't just jump right into programming without first properly tackling the fundamentals. Without knowing the fundamentals and theory behind how AR projects work, we would not be able to fully understand how the technology works or how to take advantage of some of the more abstract features of the technology. This doesn't mean that you wouldn't be able to use the technology, just that there are many underlying features that would be difficult to grasp at more advanced levels.

This book and its code files are set up with the experienced programmer in mind. There are optimization strategies employed and esoteric language constructs used that beginner programmers may not immediately understand. If you have not been studying programming for at least two years and have not used C# extensively during that period, I suggest having a reference manual or two at hand in order to clarify any programming terms or syntax usage that you are unfamiliar with. Some of the best sources for really diving into the C# language are the C# Language Specification (`https://www.ecma-international.org/publications/files/ECMA-ST/Ecma-334.pdf`) and *Learning C# By Developing Games with Unity 2017* (`https://www.packtpub.com/game-development/learning-c-7-developing-games-unity-2017-third-edition`).

Please be aware that at least two projects in this book will require the use of Xcode and will require a macOS and iOS device to compile and run properly. If you do not have, at the bare minimum, a 2011 model or later macOS, you should skip implementing the examples in the chapters and sections that deal with ARKit entirely, as you will not be able to follow along with the book. Feel free to read the sections, though, as there is always something to learn, even if you can't follow the examples.

The version of Unity3D we will be using for this book is Unity 2017.2.0f3 (64-bit) for both Windows 10 and macOS. We will be using Windows 10 version 1703 build number 15063.726 to build for Android, and macOS High Sierra (version 10.13) for building for iOS, as these are the latest versions of both operating systems at the time of writing this book.

The core information we will go over is as follows:

- Which AR toolkits are available for usage
- How to get started with each toolkit
- What the pros and cons of each toolkit are
- Reasons for developing AR applications and games

Available AR packages

Unity3D has several options readily available via plugins for creating AR applications and games:

- Vuforia AR Starter Kit
- ARCore (Tango)
- ARToolKit
- ARKit

It should be noted that Vuforia Starter Kit has been fully integrated into Unity3D and is quite easy to jump right into creating projects with. ARKit and ARCore, however, are slightly different. Because they are still in the experimental and early developmental phases, Apple and Google have not released full and proper SDKs for Unity Technologies to incorporate into the engine.

There is a plugin that exists for both of them that you will have to compile to get it to work with your project for Apple and Android devices, and we will go into how to compile and integrate into Unity3D to get it to work appropriately later in this chapter. For now, it is good to know that there is a little bit more setup involved with getting AR to work with iOS and Android.

With the introduction out of the way, we can finally begin to really talk about AR, what it is exactly, and how to set up Unity3D to take advantage of the SDKs available to create your own AR games and applications. Without further ado, let's define what AR actually is.

Defining AR

AR is augmented reality. Augmented reality is taking some form of reality and changing it in a specific way to enhance the experience. What augmented reality typically refers to is as follows:

1. Sound:

Sound perception

2. Video:

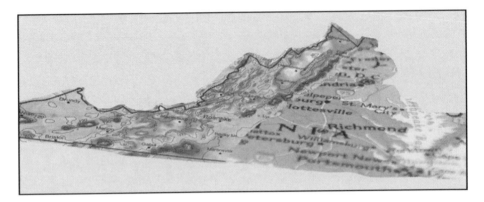

The text in this image is not important. We are just showcasing the video perception overlay

3. Graphics:

The text in this image is not important. We are just showcasing the Graphic perception overlay

4. Haptics:

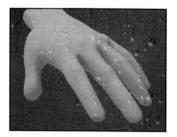

Haptic perception

5. GPS data:

GPS perception

This means that we could boost visual graphics of an object and view it in a different perspective than what we are accustomed to, or we could add something that isn't there. The video is a little bit different, as it requires the software to interface with specialized hardware, such as glasses, cell phones, HUDs, and other devices.

We could boost the auditory aspect of the world around us. We could take words we see in one language and have it say those words in another, or we could pick up those faint sounds that we always hear and tune out, then amplify them and really bring them to the forefront.

Haptic perception is a little more difficult, but it could be achieved with sensors that emulate touch. We could make something vibrate softly or harshly to simulate various effects, or we could make the game or application entirely touch- or motion-sensor-based. There are many other things we could use for haptic perception in applications or games. It is a field that is constantly being researched and expanded upon.

For GPS data, we can use the user's location to know where the user is in the app or game world. Another use for GPS data would be to know if something of interest to the user should be shown to them.

Because Unity3D loves to take care of most of the finer details of implementation for us, we don't have to worry too much about incorporating DLLs (dynamic-link libraries) or writing the wrapper classes to work with the majority of the popular AR and VR devices. There are exceptions to this rule, depending on the platform and whether the engine has been updated to specifically work with those devices.

Android and iOS are the most popular devices for applications and games to have AR incorporated into them, however, the various tech giants have been working hard to add more and more devices into the mix, with varying amounts of success. Some of these will obviously not have implementation with Unity3D, although you can write wrapper classes as previously mentioned, however, that is outside the scope of this book.

An incomplete list of AR devices

Let's take a quick look at some AR-capable devices. This should give us a slightly better idea of the different types of devices we can use and deploy to:

- The **Meta 2** is a head-mounted display headset that uses a sensory array for hand interactions and positional tracking, it has a visual field view of 90 degrees, and a resolution of 2560 x 1440:

Meta 2

- AR displays can be rendered on devices resembling eyeglasses, such as the **Google Glass**:

Google Glass

- Another such device is the HoloLens:

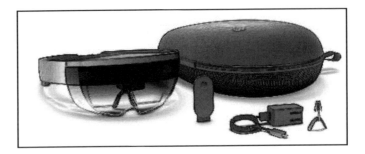

HoloLens

- There is something called a **head-up display**, which is commonly referred to as a **HUD**. It is an alternate implementation of AR displays:

HUD

- There are many new devices being researched on and created all the time. Augmented reality is still in its infancy.

All throughout this book, we will create applications and games that are inspired by the definition of AR. Since there are four main aspects of AR, we will use those four aspects and create a specific application or game for that chapter. Since we have a finite number of sensors that are available for Android and iOS devices, some sensors will be utilized in multiple projects.

Advantages and disadvantages of the different AR toolkits available

In this section, we will discuss the advantages and disadvantages of ARCore, Vuforia, ARToolKit, and ARKit.

ARCore

ARCore is a platform for building augmented reality apps for Android devices. ARCore uses three key technologies to integrate virtual content with the world through the camera. It uses motion tracking, environmental understanding, and light estimation. ARCore works by tracking the position of the device as it moves and builds its own understanding of the real world. It is able to identify interesting points and readings from the phone's sensors and has the ability to determine both the position and the orientation of the phone as it moves. ARCore only has a few supported devices at the present time, which are as follows:

- Google Pixel
- Pixel XL
- Pixel 2
- Pixel 2 XL
- Samsung Galaxy S8

If you don't own one of these devices, you are stuck using the Android Emulator for testing purposes. This is a very obvious downside, since not everyone owns one of these specific phones; additionally, the Android Emulator is an experimental piece of software and is subject to change often. The upside is that ARCore works with Unity3D and Unreal Engine as well as native to Android devices using the Java programming language.

ARKit

ARKit, which was introduced in iOS 11, is a framework for easily creating augmented reality projects for the iPhone and iPad. ARKit's features include:

- TrueDepth Camera
- Visual Inertial Odometry
- Scene Understanding
- Lighting Estimation
- Rendering Optimizations

The downsides to ARKit are that it is an experimental software and subject to change often, and that it requires the use of the Apple iPhone X to take full advantage of the TrueDepth Camera. You cannot compile this on Windows for Mac, so it is a requirement to have a macOS to even test the code properly. The pros, however, are that ARKit works with Unity3D and Unreal Engine and can utilize the A9, A10, and A11 Apple processors. In other words, it works with the iPhone 6S and beyond.

Vuforia

Vuforia is one of the most popular platforms to help you work with augmented reality development. It supports the following:

- Android
- iOS
- UWP
- Unity3D Editor

Vuforia is able to do many different things, such as recognition of different types of visual objects (such as boxes, cylinders, and planes), text and environment recognition, and VuMark, which is a combination of picture and QR code. Also, using the Vuforia Object Scanner, you can scan and create object targets. The recognition process can be implemented using the database (local or cloud storage). The Unity plugin is simple to integrate and very powerful. All plugins and functionalities of the platform are free to use but include the Vuforia watermarks.

The limitations just relate to the number of VuMarks and the amount of Cloud recognition:

- Paid plan without watermarks
- 1,000 Cloud recognitions
- 100,000 targets
- Costs $99 per month

The obvious downside is that this is not 100% free software, although they do have a developer tier with 1,000 cloud recognitions and 1,000 targets for free per month.

ARToolKit

ARToolKit is an open source tracking library for AR projects. It is supported on Android, iOS, Linux, and macOS. ARToolKit has the functionality to utilize the following:

- Single or stereo camera for position/orientation tracking
- Tracking of simple black squares
- Tracking of planar images
- Camera calibration
- Optical stereo calibration
- Optical head-mounted display support

It is fast enough for real-time AR applications. It is also free and open source software, with plugins for Unity and OpenSceneGraph. The downside to this software is that it has a huge variety of functions, so it is difficult to integrate the library, and it takes more time to explore all the available options and settings.

Building our first AR applications

This section will define all the main points of each of the different SDKs available to us, and we will build our first program with them. This will be in a step-by-step and very in-depth tutorial design sort of way, since this is a lot of information to package and condense into a small section without needing to reiterate the information in later chapters.

Setting up Vuforia

It is now time to set up a Unity3D project for each of the different SDKs that will serve as the basis for later chapters when we use each of them to build an application or a game. Let's start with Vuforia, since it is the simplest one to set up:

1. We now need to register with Vuforia. Navigate to `https://developer.vuforia.com/vui/user/register` in order to go to the registration landing page. If you live in a country in which Google is blocked, you should use a VPN, because the registration page uses the Google-powered reCAPTCHA and you can't continue without it:

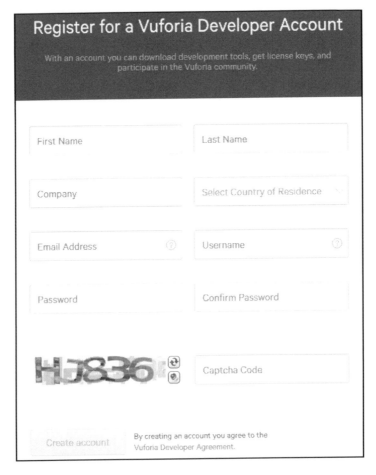

Registering on Vuforia

2. Once you can log in, navigate to the **Develop** tab; alternatively, follow this link: `https://developer.vuforia.com/targetmanager/licenseManager/licenseListing`.

3. You will see two main items, **License Manager** and **Target Manager**. The License Manager will allow you to create a free Development Key or purchase a Development Key. We want to create a free one. Click on **Get Development Key**. Enter a name for the app, which you can change at any time. I shall call mine `VuforiaIntro`:

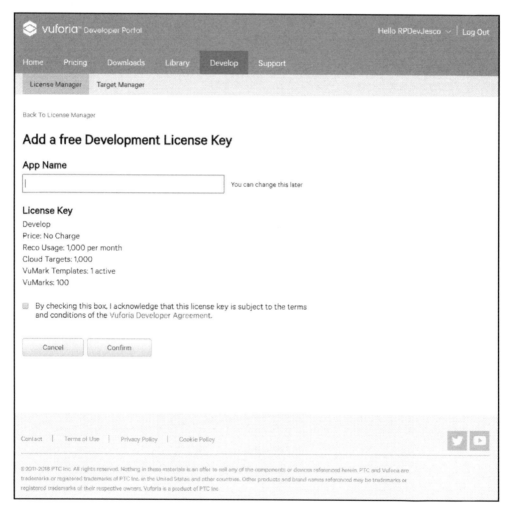

Adding a Vuforia key

4. Now, we have our key with Vuforia. In order to see the license key, we need to click on the name of our app:

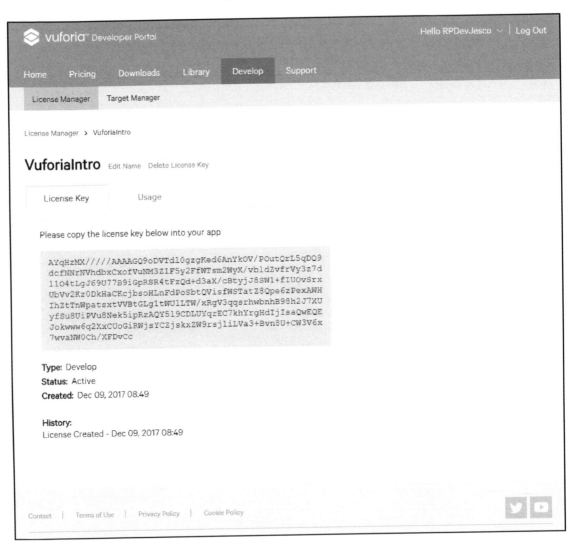

Vuforia key info

5. This next page gives us two very important pieces of information: **License Key** and **Usage** details. The **Usage** details tells us how many Cloud recognitions, Cloud databases, Recognitions used, Cloud targets used, VuMarks generated, VuMark databases, VuMark templates, and VuMarks we have used or currently have remaining:

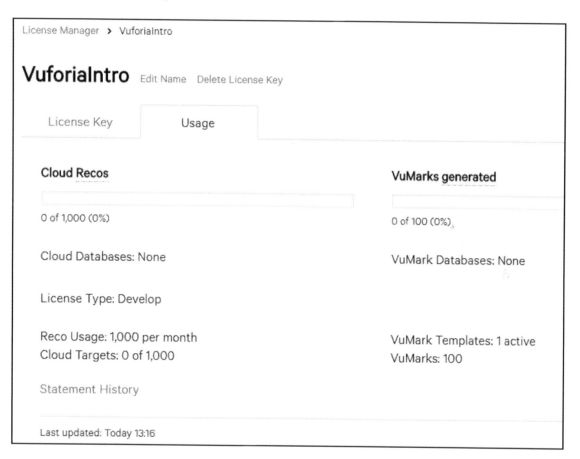

6. The **License Key** details tell us our key (which is easy to copy to the clipboard), the type of key it is, the status of the key, the date it was created, and the history of the key.

Now, we are ready to set up Vuforia and get the demo project working appropriately.

As stated previously, Vuforia is fully integrated into Unity3D as of 2017.2, and is a dream to work with once you learn the basics of the SDK. Vuforia is made to strictly deal with the graphics portion of AR. It can recognize images and objects, and it has the ability to interact with the real world, because it uses computer vision. Since Vuforia is built into Unity3D, we will do the installation of Unity with Vuforia all in one go.

If you don't have Unity3D installed on your computer now, let's go ahead and do that:

1. Navigate to `http://www.Unity3D.com` and download the latest Personal edition (or one of the others, if you are a high roller) installer for Unity:

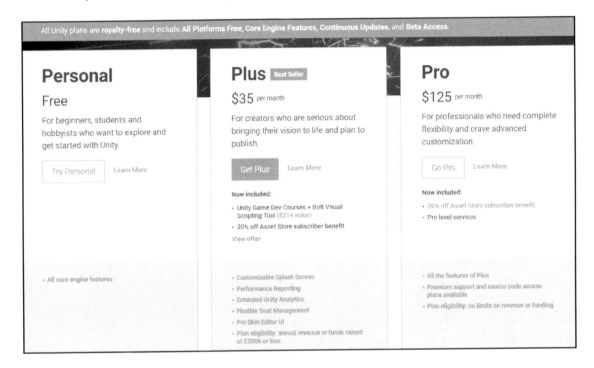

2. When you get to the components section of the installer, make sure to select all the platforms you want to support. I typically select **Android Build Support**, **Linux Build Support, SamsungTV Build Support, Tizen Build Support, WebGL Build Support**, and **UWP (Universal Windows Platform) Build Support**. There is one additional one you need to make sure you select, and that is **Vuforia Augmented Reality Support**:

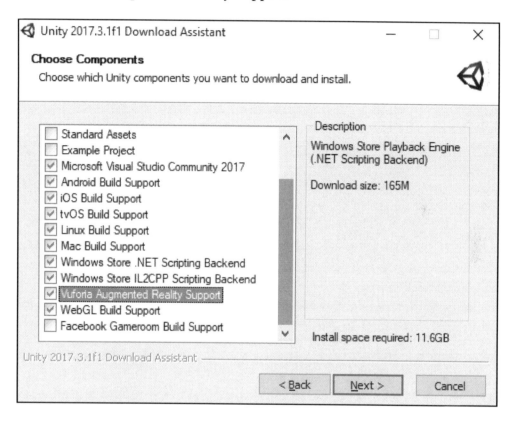

Vuforia Unity installation

Now that Unity3D has been installed, let's create a brand new Unity project:

1. Vuforia recommends that you use a 3D project setup for their AR apps, so, with that in mind, I will keep it as a 3D project with Enable Unity Analytics disabled, and the name of the project shall be `VuforiaIntro`:

2. Once the project has loaded, we can take a look at some of the additional editor items we have access to now. In the toolbar at the top of the Unity Editor, we will see **File**, **Edit**, **Assets**, **GameObject**, **Component**, **Window**, and **Help**:

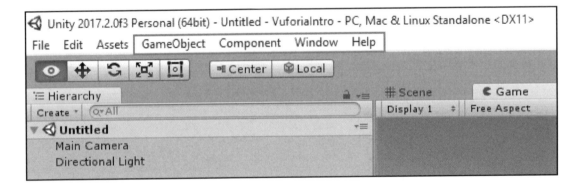

3. **GameObject**, **Component**, **Window**, and **Help** have additional items added to them. Looking at **GameObject**, we can see that the additional item is **Vuforia**. Inside the **Vuforia** item, we have **AR Camera**, **Image**, **Multi Image**, **Cylindrical Image**, **Cloud Image**, **Camera Image**, **VuMark**, and **3D Scan**:

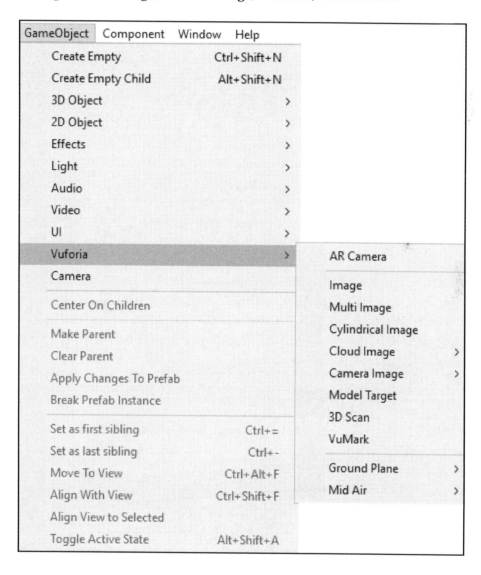

4. **Cloud Image** has some additional items, so let's take a look at that. We have **Cloud Provider** and **Cloud Image Target** available to us:

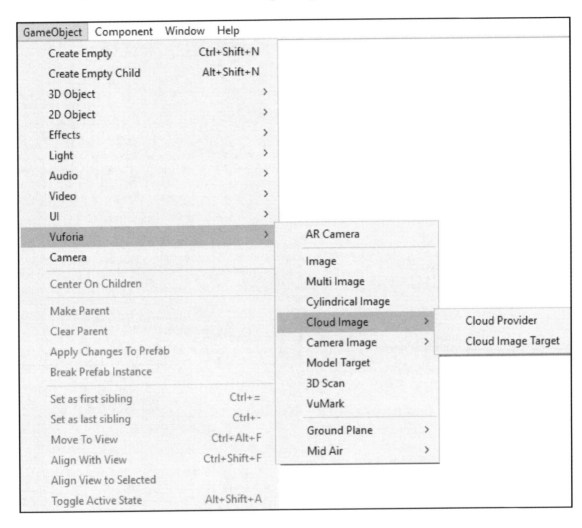

5. **Camera Image** also has some additional items, so we should also be familiar with those options. The options available are **Camera Image Builder** and **Camera Image Target**:

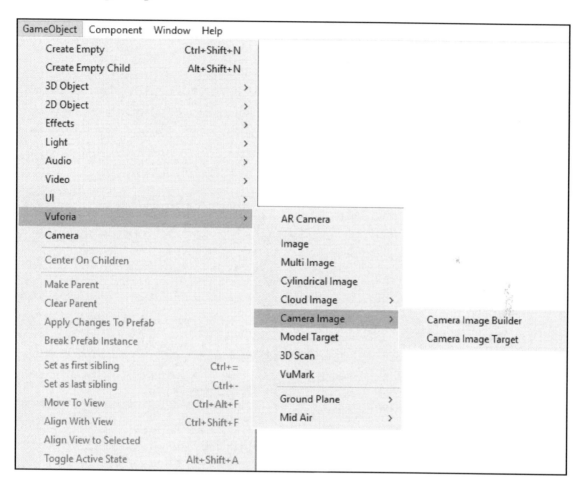

Before we go any further, we should know exactly what these options do and how they look when added to the project prior to the license being applied.

AR Camera replaces the standard camera, as it has the base camera component and **Audio Listener** components. We also see that it has two scripts attached, **Vuforia Behavior** and **Default Initialization Error Handler**:

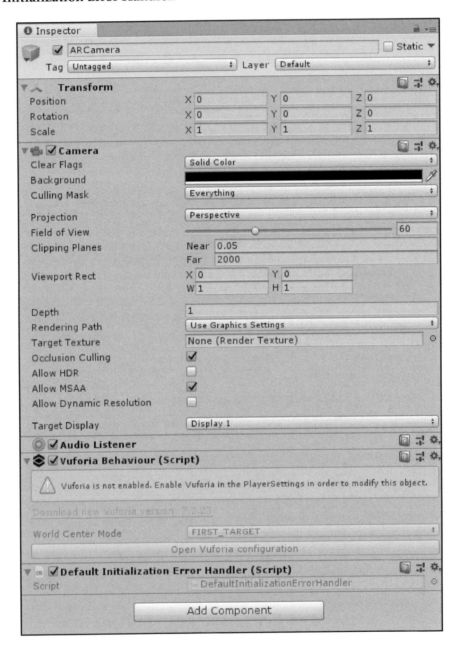

- **Image** is what allows you to add a trackable object into your AR project and serves as the basis for allowing you to have a mount point for bringing models into the camera feed.
- **Multi Image** allows you to add multiple trackable objects into your AR project and serves as the anchor for bringing models into the camera feed in real time.
- **Cylindrical Image** is an anchor for images wrapped onto objects that are cylindrical in shape.
- **VuMark** is a custom barcode made by the Vuforia team. It allows you to encode data into it as well as act as an AR target like the Image, Multi Image, and Cylindrical Image.
- **Cloud Provider** is a direct link to your cloud database for specialized AR-designed branding. It is supposed to be used for publications (catalogs, magazines, newspapers, and so on), retailers (product visualization and in-store traffic generation), advertisers (multi-branded content, coupons, and promotions), and product recognition (wine labels/ bottles, cereal boxes, and so on).
- **Cloud Image Target** is what allows you to add a trackable object into the AR project and serves as the anchor for the app to send the recognized data to the cloud database to retrieve the information and display it as you wish.
- **Camera Image Builder** is what allows you to define a target image to be stored in a database for retrieval and usage in an AR application.
- **Camera Image Target** serves as the anchor for which to use the self-defined target image to display what you want on screen when recognized.

The next set of items to talk about is in the **Component** toolbar. The special components lie within the **AR**, **Scripts**, and **XR** portions of the **Component** window, as marked in the following screenshot for reference. In order to use them, you have to have a **GameObject** in the scene and add the component from the toolbar to it. We have **World Anchor**, **Tracked Pose Driver**, **Spatial Mapping Collider**, and **Spatial Mapping Renderer** available. We should do a deep dive in so that we can know exactly what these items do:

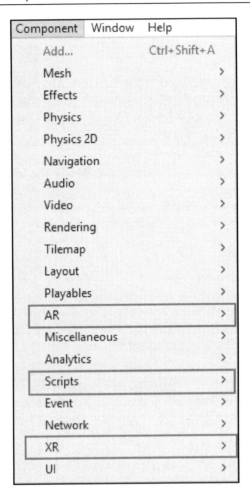

- **World Anchor** is a component that represents a link between an exact point in the physical world and the parent GameObject of the World Anchor. Once added, a GameObject with a World Anchor component remains locked in place to locations in the real world.
- **Tracked Pose Driver** is a component that applies the current Pose value of a tracked device to the transform of the Game Object.
- **Spatial Mapping Collider** allows for holographic content (or character) interaction, such as physics, with the spatial mapping mesh.
- **Spatial Mapping Renderer** is a component that gives a visual representation of Spatial Mapping surfaces. This is useful for visually debugging surfaces and adding visual effects to the environment.

It should be noted that there are items related to Vuforia in the **Scripts** section, however, we will not cover those here. But, just for the sake of making sure that the items are listed, they are as follows:

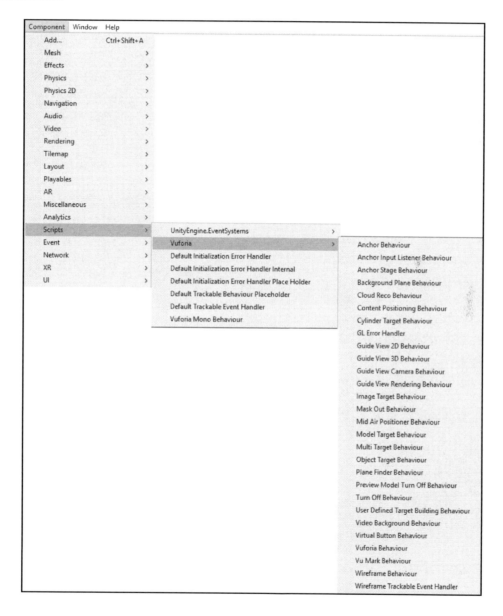

- Background Plane Behaviour
- Cloud Reco Behaviour
- Cylinder Target Behaviour
- GL Error Handler
- Image Target Behaviour
- Mask Out Behaviour
- Multi Target Behaviour
- Object Target Behaviour
- Prop Behaviour
- Reconstruction Behaviour
- Reconstruction From Target Behaviour
- Surface Behaviour
- Text Reco Behaviour
- Turn Off Behaviour
- Turn off Word Behaviour
- User Defined Target Building Behaviour
- Video Background Behaviour
- Virtual Button Behaviour
- Vuforia Behaviour
- Vuforia Deinit Behaviour
- Vu Mark Behaviour
- Wireframe Behaviour
- Wireframe Trackable Event Handler
- Word Behaviour

In the **Inspector** pane, we have Vuforia Configuration. The following is a screenshot of it; next, we will define what it does:

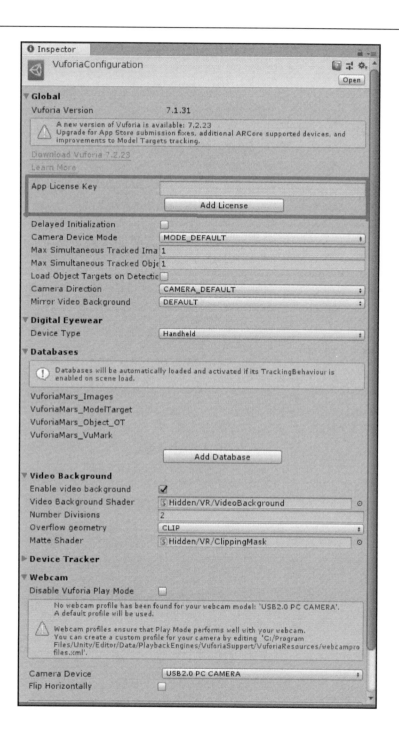

Vuforia Configuration allows you to enter your License Key. Clicking on **Add License** will load the Vuforia Developer landing page. It also allows you to specify what you want Vuforia to be configured to work for, such as a HUD, smartglasses, a webcam, or a smartphone.

 I also want to note that Smart Terrain Tracker has been deprecated and will be removed in the next release of Vuforia. If you are reading this book and that screenshot does not look the same, you now know why and should not be worried.

Since we are here, let's go ahead and add our app key to Vuforia (see Vuforia Add License for its location):

1. You should create your own app key, since my app key will not be valid by the time of the release of this book. After copying and pasting your key into the license key box, just press the *Return/Enter* key and you are done:

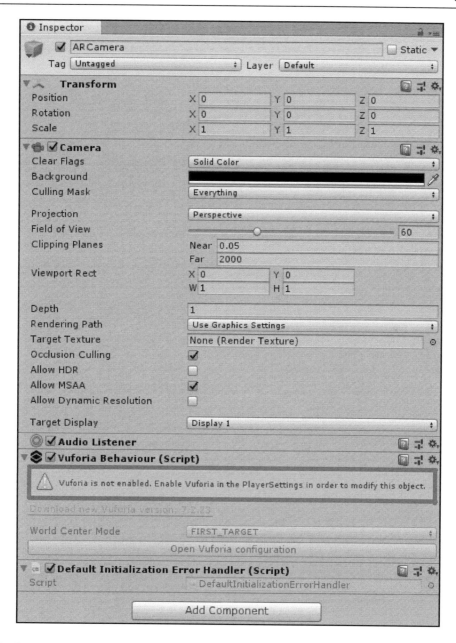

2. Since we are testing on PC and if you have a webcam that works for said PC, make sure that the **Camera Device** selects the proper webcam for usage:

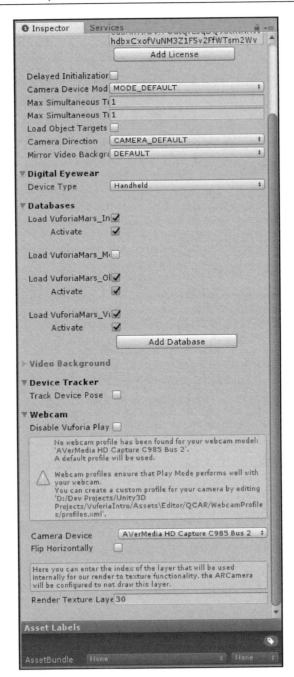

3. Next, we need to go into the Unity Player Settings and fix some options. Navigate to **File** and click on **Build Settings**. The **Build Settings** box should appear. Make sure you change the project type to build to **Android**, and then click on **Player Settings**:

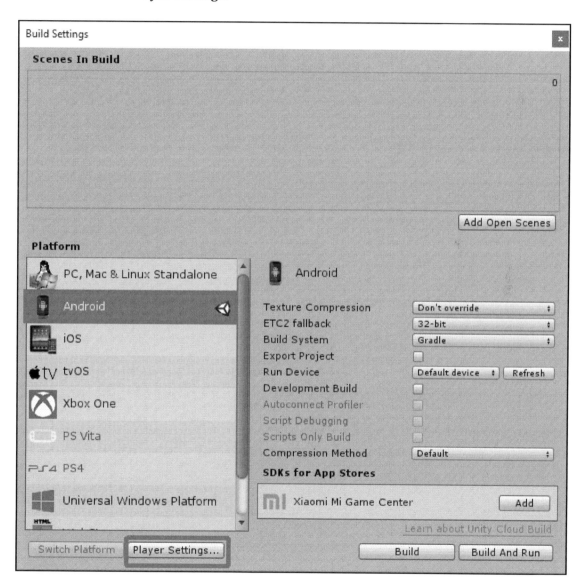

4. Vuforia does not support **FAT device filter** or **Android TV**, so we need to change those two options. **Device Filter**, which is located in **Other Settings**, needs to be changed to **ARMv7**, and **Android TV Compatibility** needs to be unchecked.

5. Now, we can finally build our "Hello World" AR application for testing to make sure Vuforia and Unity3D are working well together. If you haven't done so already, remove the regular camera component from the **Hierarchy** Pane and replace it with the **ARCamera**:

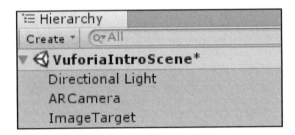

6. The next step is to add the Vuforia Image to the scene, which is also known as the **ImageTarget**:

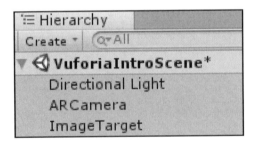

7. We now need to download and add a 3D model to the scene. So, let's go with the easy route and just add a sphere to the scene with the *x*, *y*, and *z* scale set to 0.3. Take extra special care to make sure that the sphere is a child of the **ImageTarget**. *This is very important*:

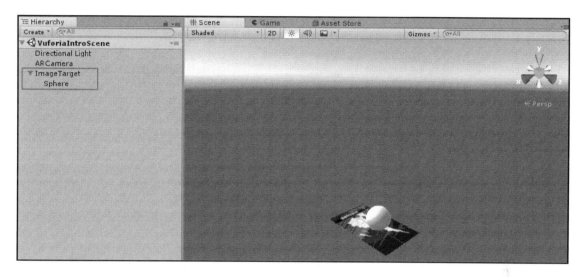

8. The next step is to navigate to **Editor | Vuforia | ForPrint | ImageTargets**, and print out on a piece of paper `target_images_A4` or `target_images_USLetter`:

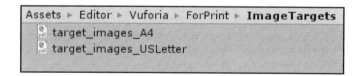

9. Once you have it printed, we can begin the final portion of the test, which is to run the program and hold the printout of the drone in front of the webcam:

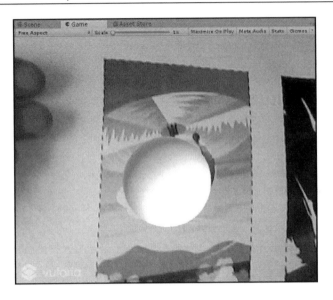

The text in this screenshot is not important. It shows a sphere that appears on the camera feed when the image is recognized.

10. Vuforia has now been properly configured and tested appropriately, so we can move on to the next SDK to set up and configure.

Setting up ARToolKit

ARToolKit is a bit more difficult to set up and get started with.

 ARToolKit has been depreciated and is now part of the Daqri Vos API. which you can view
at https://developer.daqri.com/#!/content/develop
This section has been kept in for incase you want to utilize ARToolkit from the github link https://github.com/artoolkit/arunity5

There are two different ways you can get ARToolKit in a project and ready to develop with. The first option is the easiest, and that is through the Asset Store: https://assetstore. unity.com/packages/tools/artoolkit-6-unitypackage-94863. This is the latest version of ARToolKit in the Asset Store and it will be imported directly into Unity for you. The other option is to go to the main website of ARToolKit: https://github.com/artoolkit/ artoolkit5. This allows you to get additional tools and the actual SDK, along with the Unity Package.

For installation into Unity3D, we will go with the second option, since it is less intuitive than the first option:

1. Navigate to the main website for ARToolKit and click on **DOWNLOAD SDK**. The macOS, Windows, iOS, Android, Linux, Windows 8.1, and Source Dependencies don't need to be downloaded, but they can be if you want to go deeper into how ARToolKit works under the hood or if you want to use it in a non-Unity capacity. Instead, head toward the bottom of the page and click on the **DOWNLOAD UNITY PACKAGE** button:

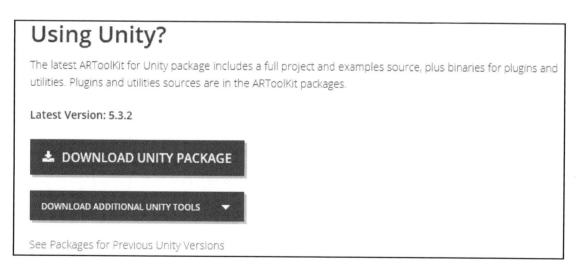

Unless you are doing something more involved, you don't need the additional Unity tools at the present time if you are on a macOS, but if you are on a PC, I suggest getting the Windows Tools, since ARToolKit needs them to debug on PC without using the Android Emulator or testing on Linux.

2. Now that the package has been downloaded, we need to open Unity3D and create a new project. I will call mine `ARToolKitIntro`. Keep the settings as default for simplicity's sake:

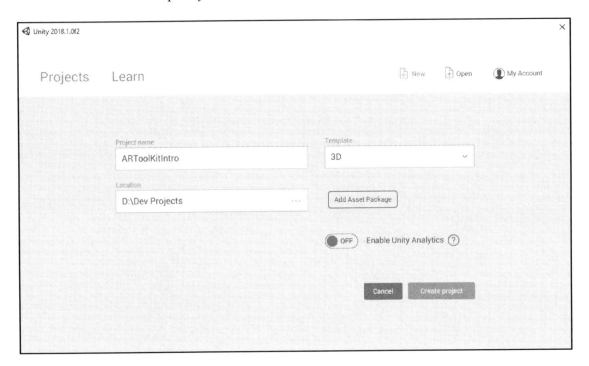

3. Now, we need to import the Unity Package into Unity. This is pretty straightforward. Right-click the `Assets` folder, highlight **Import Package**, and select **Custom Package**:

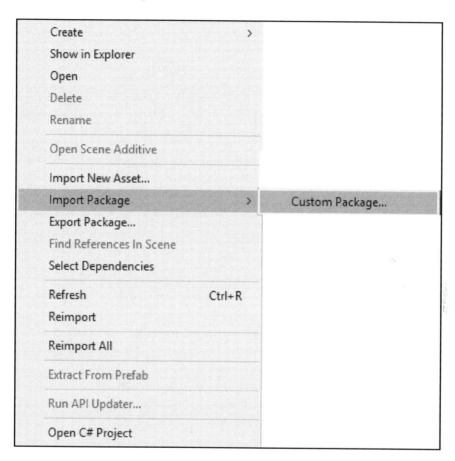

4. Navigate to the folder that houses the downloaded Unity Package, click on it, and select **Open**. You should see a dialog box with checkboxes inside. Click on **All** and then click on **Import**:

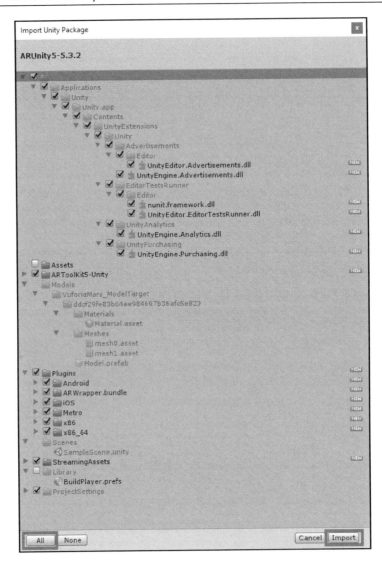

5. You will see three folders after the import is complete (ARToolKit5-Unity, Plugins, and StreamingAssets):

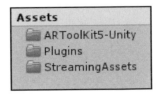

Inside the `ARToolKit5-Unity` folder, there are the `Example Scenes`, `Examples`, `Materials`, `Resources`, `Scripts`, `Changelog`, and `Readme` files and folders:

- Inside `Scripts`, we have an `Editor` folder with the features shown in the following screenshot:

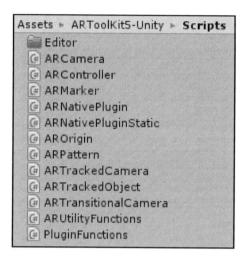

- Inside the `Editor` folder, we have the following:

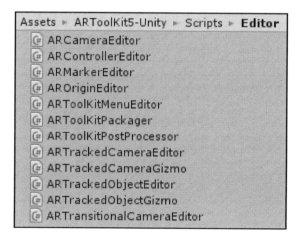

- Next up is the `Plugins` folder. It has folders listed as follows:

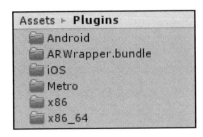

- If you look at the menu bar at the top of the Unity Editor, you will see an additional toolbar item: **ARToolKit**. The drop-down menu shows several options: **ARToolKit for Unity Version 5.3.2**, **Download Tools**, **Build**, **Support**, and **Source Code**:

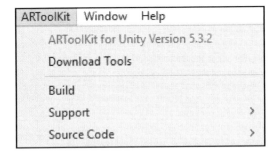

- **Support** has **Home Page**, **Documentation**, and **Community Forums**:

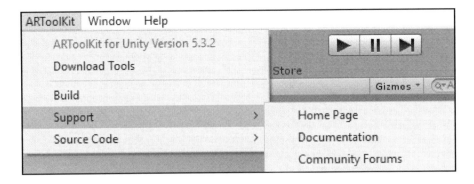

- **Source Code** has **View ARToolKit Source** and **View Unity Plugin Source**:

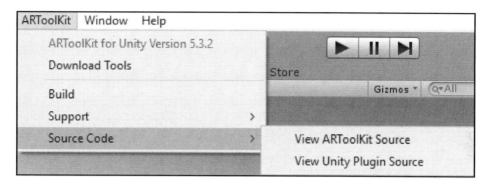

The basics are out of the way, so we can begin building our "Hello World" with ARToolKit:

1. The first thing we need to do is create an empty game object in the **Hierarchy** pane and rename it ARToolKit.

2. The next step is to add the ARController script to the game object and delete the Camera:

3. The ARController script handles the creation and management of AR tracking. It automatically adds a camera at runtime and is controlled by the user layers that we provide.

4. With this latest version of ARToolKit, the basic user layers are provided for you already: AR background, AR background 2, and AR foreground for **User Layer 8**, **User Layer 9**, and **User Layer 10**, respectively:

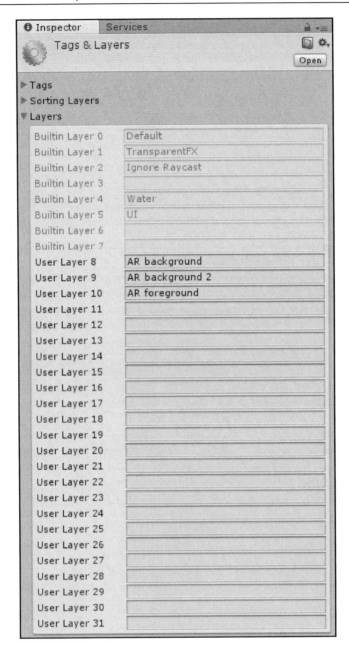

5. The **AR Controller** script has a **Video Options** drop-down menu:

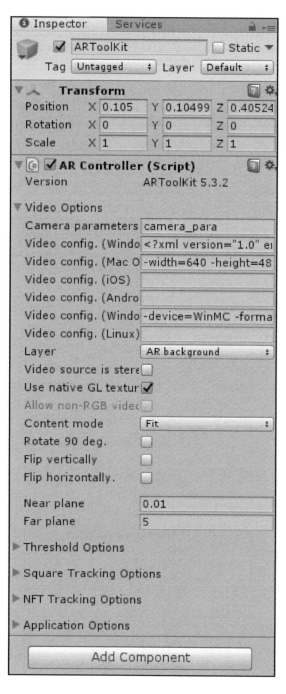

6. Since we have so many different options for video, we need to set it up properly:

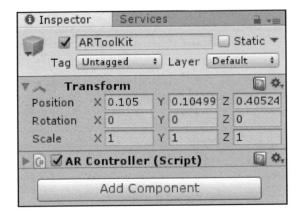

7. If you get errors in the console of the Unity Editor, then you don't have the latest version of ARToolKit with the version of Unity we are using in this book.

Since I am building for Windows, I will go to the first option of Video config and input the following:

```
<?xml version="1.0" encoding="utf-8"?>
<dsvl_input>
<camera show_format_dialog="false" frame_width="1280" frame_height="720"
frame_rate="29.97">
<pixel_format>
<RGB32 flip_v="true"/>
</pixel_format>
</camera>
</dsvl_input>
```

Now, since my computer does not presently have a webcam attached to it, I get an in-game error message, but the code compiles and runs as expected. If you have a webcam attached and it is recognized appropriately, you should have a direct feed from your webcam.

This concludes the Hello World for ARToolKit; we will be revisiting this one later on for more in-depth and fun usage of this SDK.

Setting up ARCore

ARCore and ARKit are fundamentally very similar, but you can't compile ARKit on a Windows environment, which is what I'm presently using. Not to worry; when we get to ARKit, I will be using a macOS to give you a proper view and feel of how things are when using it.

That being said, it is now time to take a deeper look at ARCore.

ARCore was made by Google and is currently in the early preview stages; it hasn't even reached release 1.0 yet, so there are bound to be many changes, some of which could be extremely damaging to existing apps or games.

There are two ways to get the SDK preview for Unity. The first is through a Unity Package file (`https://developers.google.com/ar/develop/unity/quickstart-android`) and the other is through GitHub (`https://github.com/google-ar/arcore-unity-sdk`). Now, since I have been having an issue with downloading from Amazon Web Services lately, I will use the second link:

Setting up your development environment

- Install the Android SDK version 7.0 (API Level 24) or higher.
  - To install the Android SDK, install Android Studio.
  - To update the Android SDK, use the Android SDK Manager tool in Android Studio.
- Install Unity 2017.3.0f2 or higher, with the **Android Build Support** component. For more info, see Downloading and Installing Unity ⬈.
- You will need to get the ARCore SDK for Unity. You can either:
  - Download the SDK for Unity and extract it.

    -or-

  - Clone the repository with the following command:

    ```
    $ git clone https://github.com/google-ar/arcore-unity-sdk.git
    ```

- You will need a supported Android device.

It is key to remember that, if you don't have a Samsung Galaxy 8 or a Google Pixel phone, you will not be able to run proper tests on your device. However, if you also install Android Studio, you do get access to the Android Emulator:

1. To begin, create a new project in Unity and call it ARCoreTutorial:

2. We need to change the **Build Settings** to **Android** before doing anything else:

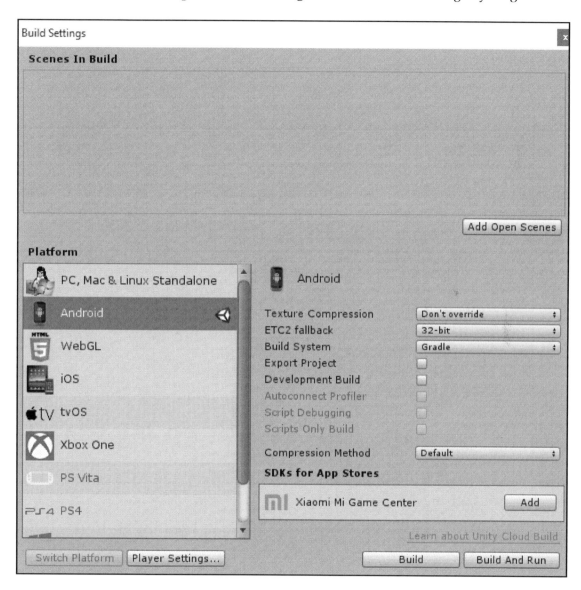

3. Next up, we need to change the **Player Settings**. The main settings we need to change are within the **Other Settings** tab, so let's take a look at what needs to be changed.

4. Other Settings: We want **Multithreaded Rendering** unchecked; **Minimum API Level** should be **Android 7.0 'Nougat' API level 24**; and **Target API Level** should be **Android 7.0 'Nougat' API level 24** or **Android 7.1 'Nougat' API level 25**:

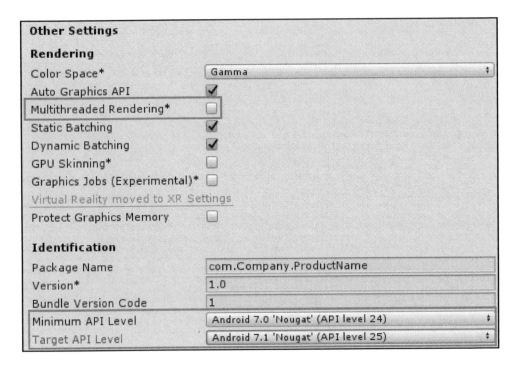

5. **XR Settings**: We want **ARCore Supported** to be checked:

6. Next up, we want to unzip the SDK or import the package into Unity3D:

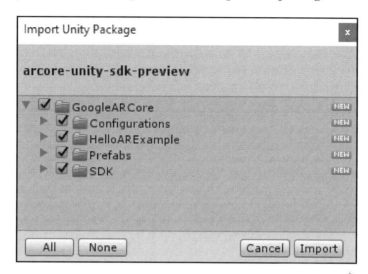

Right away, we should see a **DLLNotFoundException** for `tango_client_api2`. This is normal and is well-known by the community. It should not cause any errors at runtime, though; it should be fixed in a later release.

Setting up ARKit

ARKit requires the usage of macOS High Sierra, because of the XCode 9 and above requirement for compiling and making changes to the API itself. So, I would highly suggest having a macOS from late 2011 or newer. I am utilizing a Mac Mini 2011 model with 8 GB of RAM, although the standard 4 GB should be plenty. Unity3D does utilize OpenCL/OpenGL extensively, which requires a GFX card capable of utilizing Metal. 2011 and earlier macOSs do not have this ability natively; this could be circumvented by having an external GPU (Radeon RX 480 is currently the only GPU supported officially for this).

With that out of the way, we can begin with installing and configuring ARKit for Unity3D on our macOS.

There are a couple of ways you can install ARKit:

1. We can navigate to the plugin page on the Asset Store (`https://www.assetstore.unity3d.com/en/#!/content/92515`):

2. Or we can download the plugin directly from the Bitbucket repository (`https://bitbucket.org/Unity-Technologies/unity-arkit-plugin/overview`):

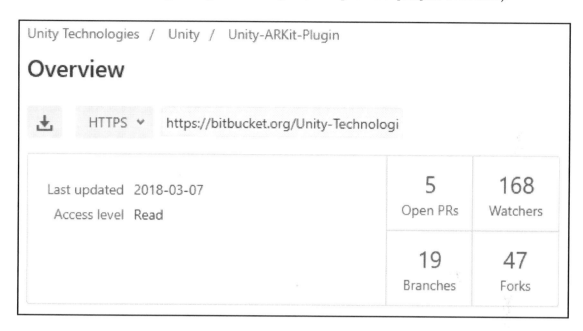

3. If we go the first route and install from the Asset Store, we don't have to worry about copying the files into our project ourselves, but either way it is simple enough to do, so take your pick on the method you want to go with and create a new project called ARKitTutorial:

Next up, we have quite a bit to unpack regarding what is actually in this package:

- /Assets/Plugins/iOs/UnityARKit/NativeInterface/ARsessionNative. mm – This is the Objective-C code that is the actual interfaces with the ARKit SDK.
- /Assets/Plugins/iOS/UnityARKit/NativeInterface/UnityARSessionNa tiveInterface.cs – This is the scripting API that glues the native code to ARKit.
- /Assets/Plugins/iOS/UnityARKit/NativeInterface/AR*.cs – These are the equivalents of the data structures exposed by ARKit.
- /Assets/Plugins/iOS/UnityARKit/Utility/UnityARAnchorManager.cs – This is a utility script that tracks the anchor updates from ARKit and can create the proper corresponding GameObjects in Unity for them.
- /Assets/Plugins/iOS/UnityARKit/Editor/UnityARBuildPostprocessor .cs – This is an editor script that runs at build time on iOS.

- `/Assets/Plugins/iOS/UnityARKit/UnityARCameraManager.cs` – This is the component that should be placed on a GameObject in the scene that references the camera that you want to control. It will position and rotate the camera as well as provide the correct projection matrix based on updates from ARKit. This component also initializes as ARKit Session.
- `/Assets/Plugins/iOS/UnityARKit/UnityARVideo.cs` – This is the component that should be placed on the camera and grabs the textures needed for rendering the video. It sets the material needed for blitting to the backbuffer and sets up the command buffer for blitting.
- `/Assets/Plugins/iOS/UnityARKit/UnityARUserAnchorComponent.cs` – This is the component that adds and removes Anchors from ARKit based on the life cycle of the GameObject it is added to.

Before we build our own "Hello World" example, we should build the `UnityARKitScene.unity` to iOS to get a taste of what ARKit is capable of, as it demonstrates all of the basic functionality of ARKit in that scene.

`UnityARKitScene` is included in the plugin as well as a couple of other example projects. We will compile the `UnityARKitScene` as our Hello World application.

However, before we do that, we need to talk about the file structure, because those who are not well-versed with compiling to iOS will have some serious issues compiling without further clarification. You may have noticed quite a few items that we have not mentioned that are in the plugin, so let's go ahead and discuss what all of them do before moving on.

`\UnityARKitPlugin` main directory files:

- `ARKitRemote` – Allows you to send remote commands from your device to the Unity3D editor
- `Examples` – This directory houses example scripts and scenes to showcase various things you can do with ARKit and this plugin
- `Plugins` – Houses the directories required to run ARKit
- `Resources` – Houses the resource files required for ARKit

`Plugins\iOS\UnityARKit\NativeInterface` cs files:

- `ARAnchor` – Anchors an object to a location in the world from the camera feed.
- `ARCamera` – Tracks the camera's position.
- `ARErrorCode` – Error codes.
- `ARFaceAnchor` – Face tracking anchor.

- `ARFrame` – Returns data about the camera, anchors, and light estimates.
- `ARHitTestResult` –Returns any collision results.
- `ARHitTestResultType` – Enumeration for the hit test types available.
- `ARLightEstimate` – Calculates how much luminosity is in the image or video.
- `ARPlaneAnchor` – Anchors a plane to a specific 4x4 matrix.
- `ARPlaneAnchorAlignment` – Aligns the anchor horizontally with respect to gravity.
- `ARPoint` – A point struct for x and y values as a double.
- `ARRect` – A struct that takes `ARPoint` as the origin and `ARSize` as the size.
- `ARSessionNative` – Native plugin used to specify framework dependencies and the platforms the plugin should work for.
- `ARSize` –A struct that takes a width and height value as a double.
- `ARTextureHandles` – A native Metal texture handler for the camera buffer which takes an `IntPtr` (`int pointer`) for both `textureY` and `textureCbCr` values.
- `ARTrackingQuality` – Enumeration for tracking qualities available.
- `ARTrackingState` –Enumeration for tracking states. **Limited**, **Normal**, and **NoAvailable** are the options.
- `ARTrackingStateReason` – Enumeration for the state reasons. Options are **Excessive Motion**, **Insufficient Features**, and **Initializing**.
- `ARUserAnchor` – Defines this anchor's transformation matrix for rotation, translation, and scale in world coordinates.
- `UnityARSessionNativeInterface` – Native plugin wrapper code.

`\Plugins\iOS\UnityARKit\Helpers` cs files:

- `AR3DOFCameraManager` – A helper class for 3D objects with the AR Camera
- `ARPlaneAnchorGameObject` – A class that attaches a GameObject with the `ARPlaneAnchor`
- `DontDestroyOnLoad` – Makes sure the GameObject doesn't get destroyed on load
- `PointCloudParticleExample` – Creates a point cloud particle system
- `UnityARAmbient` – A helper function for ambient lighting
- `UnityARAnchorManager` – A manager for `ARPlaneAnchorGameObjects`
- `UnityARCameraManager` – A helper class for the `ARCamera`

- `UnityARCameraNearFar` – Sets the Near Far distance of the camera appropriately
- `UnityARGeneratePlane` – Creates an `ARPlaneAnchorGameObject`
- `UnityARHitTestExample` – Tests collisions with various amounts of planes, from few to infinite
- `UnityARKitControl` – A helper class designed for creating a test `ARSession`
- `UnityARKitLightManager` – A helper class for managing the various lighting possibilities
- `UnityARMatrixOps` – A class for converting a 4x4 matrix to Euclidean space for quaternion rotation
- `UnityARUserAnchorComponent` – A helper class for creating Anchor added and removed events
- `UnityARUtility` – A helper class to do coordinate conversions from ARKit to Unity
- `UnityARVideo` – A helper function to render the video texture to the scene
- `UnityPointCloudExamples` – A helper function to draw a point cloud using particle effects

`\Plugins\iOS\UnityARKit\Shaders` shader files:

- `YUVShader` – A gamma Unlit Shader for rendering Textures
- `YUVShaderLinear` – A linear Unlit Shader for rendering Textures

`\UnityARKitPlugin\Resources` file:

- `UnityARKitPluginSettings.cs` – Is a scriptable object that toggles whether ARKit is required for the app and toggles Facetracking for the iPhone X.

`UnityARKitPlugin\ARKitRemote` files:

- `ARKitRemote.txt` – A text file that explains how to set up and use ARKitRemote
- `EditorTestScene.unity` – Test scene that should run when running `ARKitRemote`
- `UnityARKitRemote.unity` – Scene that should be compiled and installed on an applicable device
- `ARKitRemoteConnection.cs` – Used to send data from the device to the UnityEditor

- `ConnectionMessageIds` – GUIDs for the Editor Session Message
- `ConnectToEditor.cs` – Creates a network connection between the editor and the device
- `EditorHitTest` – Returns collision data from device to editor
- `ObjectSerializationExtension.cs` – An extension to convert an object to a byte array
- `SerializableObjects.cs` – Serializes Vector 4 data and a 4x4 matrix
- `UnityRemoteVideo.cs` – Connects to the editor and transfers a video feed from the device to the editor

`UnityARKitPlugin\Examples` files:

- `AddRemoveAnchorExample` – An example program to add and remove anchors
- `Common` – Has common materials, models, prefabs, shaders, and textures that are used in various projects
- `FaceTracking` – Face tracking example application
- `FocusSquare` – An example scene where it finds a specific anchor
- `UnityARBallz` – An example scene where you play a game with balls
- `UnityARKitScene` – A basic scene with minimal scripts attached to test if ARKit works appropriately
- `UnityAROcclusion` – An example project that showcases various lighting conditions
- `UnityARShadows` – An example project that handles low lighting conditions
- `UnityParticlePainter` – An example project that lets you paint with particles

Now that we have a fundamental understanding of everything inside this package, let's build our Hello World with ARKit.

Building Hello World in ARKit

The first thing we need to do after we open the UnityARKitScene is to set up the build settings:

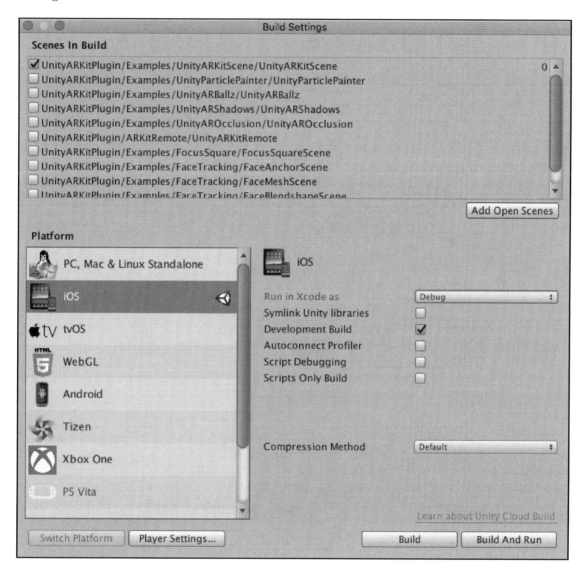

1. Click on **Build Settings** and select **Player Settings**.
2. We want to scroll down to **Identification**. The **Bundle Identifier** should be set to com.unity.ARKitHelloTutorial, **Version** to 0.1, **and Build** to 10.1. The **Automatically Sign** checkbox should be checked. Leave the **Automatic Signing Team ID** settings blank:

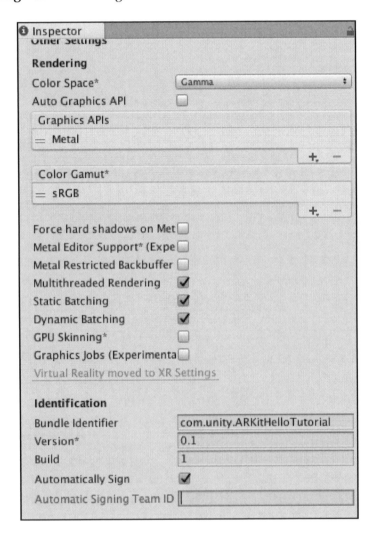

3. Build the `UnityARKitScene` for iOS only. Run Xcode in **Debug** mode.

4. Only the **Development Build** checkbox should be checked; everything else should be left as default.

5. Click **Build**. I will save the file as `iOSTest` in my data drive within a folder called `iOS`:

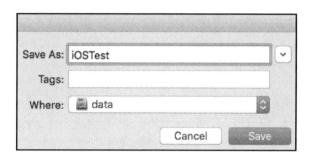

6. Building should not take very long at all, perhaps around two minutes for a first build.

7. The next thing we want to do is open the folder we saved the project in and open the `.xcodeproj` file in Xcode:

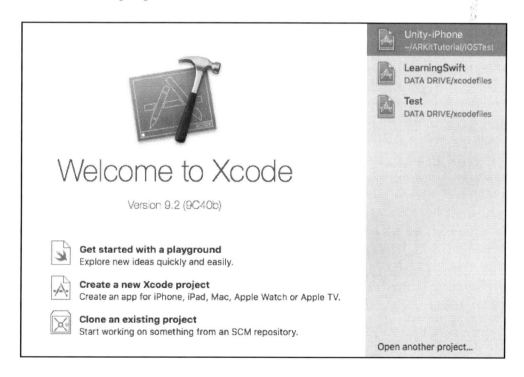

8. Let's take a look at the Base project you will see in Xcode:

9. The first thing we want to check is the **Identity** tab to make sure that these settings are the same as in Unity3D:

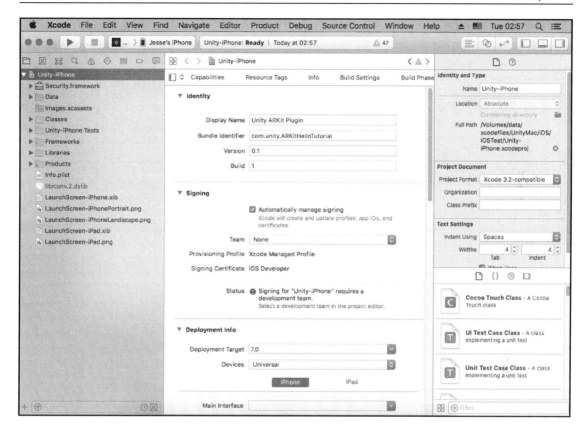

10. Now, we need to look at the **Signing** subsection:

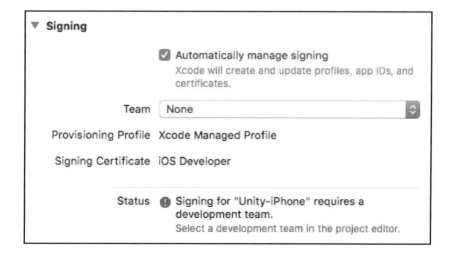

11. We need to make sure to add our Personal Team name to it, which you can get by signing in to your Apple Developer account and clicking on the arrow for the team you want to use:

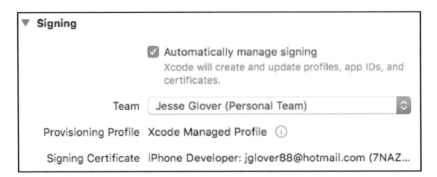

12. **Deployment Info** is next. The **Deployment Target** needs to be changed to 11.2. Devices should be set to **iPhone** only. The **Main Interface** is LaunchScreen-iPhone.xib:

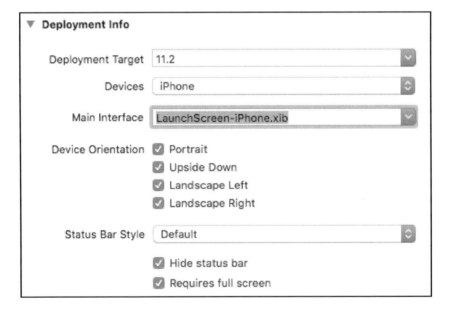

13. Click on **Build Settings** at the top, as there are a few settings we need to change here as well.

14. In **Architectures**, **ARCHS** for iPhone should be set to **Standard**. **SDKROOT** should be **Latest iOS (iOS 11.2)**. **SUPPORTED_PLATFORMS** should be **iOS**:

15. Next up, scroll down to look at signing, and the values should be already set to the correct ones:

16. Now, click on **Product** and **Build**:

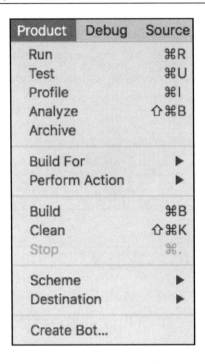

17. The build should have completed successfully with roughly 47 warnings, which is normal:

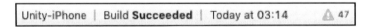

18. Now, we can build and test in the simulator. What we want to do is change from the iPhone to one of the simulators in the list, so click on the device list next to your iPhone or whatever device you have:

19. You will see a big list of devices you want to use. This will range from simulations of devices to the iOS device you have connected to your macOS:

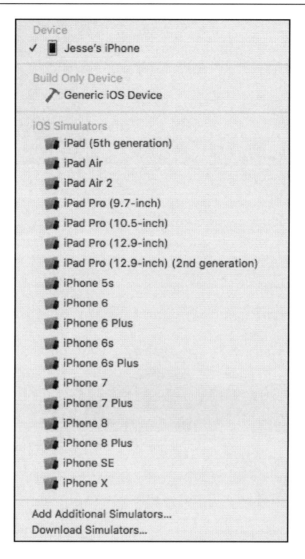

20. Click on the simulation you want to use, and then build and run the application.

Congratulations! We have completed this Hello World application.

Summary

We learned the basics of the four main AR SDKs made available to us from many companies. We installed and compiled a working example in each one of the SDKs with minimal effort, and we can now move on to utilizing these SDKs to their full potential, as they currently stand in their respective stages of development.

We can see that all four SDKs are simple enough to use and are relatively easy to install. In my opinion, the best SDK to use at the moment is Vuforia. It has the most robust API and is extremely well-documented for usage and further learning.

In the next chapter, we will focus on learning the history of GIS and how that history has shaped the way we use GIS in AR applications and games today.

Questions

1. ARView is an SDK that you can use to make AR applications in Unity:

    A.) True
    B.) False

2. ARKit is specifically designed for iOS devices only:

    A.) True
    B.) False

3. ARCore is specifically designed for Windows devices only:

    A.) True
    B.) False

4. Vuforia is designed for iOS, Windows, and Android devices:

    A.) True
    B.) False

5. Haptic perception is all about using the sense of touch:

    A.) True
    B.) False

6. Sound perception is what you see with your eyes:

    A.) True
    B.) False

7. GPS data lets the application specify the user's location by random guessing:

    A.) True
    B.) False

8. DLL files are required for Windows and Android plugins with Unity:

    A.) True
    B.) False

9. Meta 2, HoloLens, HUD, and Google Glass are all considered AR devices:

    A.) True
    B.) False

10. Vuforia is not a free SDK to use:

    A.) True
    B.) False

2
GIS Fundamentals - The Power of Mapping

When it comes to **GIS**, which is the abbreviated form of **Geographic Information Systems**, and data and usage in AR programming, it comes in many flavors and usages. However, before we get into how to use GIS data in AR games and applications, we must first understand what GIS actually is. So, we will go over things like: when GIS was developed, who the father of GIS is, where GIS can be used, and how GIS works with game and application development. The reason this is important is that the history of GIS plays directly into how data is used today in AR applications and games; it also allows us to appreciate the hard work of those in the past who made it possible for us to take advantage of readily available data online. We will go over some examples of how we can use what we have learned from the history of GIS to create applications and games later on in this chapter. The following topics will be covered in this chapter:

- Understanding what GIS is
- History of GIS and data analysis
- GIS statistics
- Implications of GIS
- GIS and AR

To understand what GIS actually is, we must dive a little deeper to discover the underlying principles of GIS and how it started. The history of GIS and data analysis is fascinating and will expose many things that allow us to understand the underlying structure of how it is set up and used. GIS statistics will allow us to be able to know which mathematical methods are commonly used so that we can take advantage of them. The implications of GIS will show us many uses of GIS, not only in academia, but also in education and real-world usage.

GIS and AR will show us some much-needed examples of how AR applications and games have incorporated GIS into them. This will give us a clear idea on what we could develop in the future.

In this chapter, we will cover the following topics:

- GIS fundamentals – the power of mapping
- GIS and augmented reality

What is GIS?

The most common definition of GIS is geographic information systems. It is comprised of a full software and hardware system that can capture geographic data and information via cameras, store it via a database, manipulate it via software, analyze it via statistical and visualization tools, and manage and present spatial or geographic data. There are other well-known defination for GIS, such as geographic information science, although that has fallen out of general use as it refers to the academic discipline that studies geographic information systems. It is not commonly used for the definition of GIS, because it is a large domain within the much broader academic discipline of geoinformatics.

This essentially boils down to the ability to describe any information system that can combine, keep for future usage, manage, examine, distribute, and manifest geographic information. In essence, you can create tools that allow for users or other tools to create two-way flows of informational queries, examine spatial data, manipulate and inspect map data, and showcase the results of all of these operations in either visual or data form.

There are many tools and a plethora of different applications related to the engineering, arrangement, administration, logistics, insurance, transport, telecommunications, and business of GIS, and due to all this, GIS and location intelligence applications are the foundations for many location-enabled services such as Google Maps, Apple Maps, Bing Maps, Pokémon Go, and many more.

The history of GIS

The first known use of the term "geographic information system" was by Roger Tomlinson in 1968. It was used in his paper called *A Geographic Information System for Regional Planning*, and because of this, he is commonly known as the "father of GIS".

The first known application for spatial analysis was in 1832 by a French geographer named Charles Picquet. He represented the 48 districts of Paris by halftone color gradients following the number of deaths incurred by the outbreak of cholera per 1,000 inhabitants.

John Snow was determined to find the source of a cholera outbreak in 1854. He attempted to find the source of the cholera outbreak in London's Broad Street region by marking points on a map to depict where the cholera victims lived, and by connecting the cluster he found, he was able to link the source of the outbreak to a water source that was nearby. This was one of the first known effective employments of geographic procedures in the study of disease transmission.

In his map, he used bars to represent deaths that occurred at specified households; however, in his first map, there were several minor errors. One of these errors was the location of the Broad Street pump:

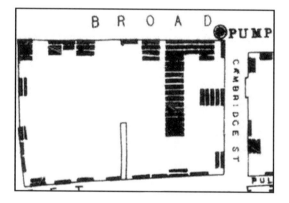

The text in this image is not important. It gives a gist of John Snow's first map

With the second map he published, he fixed his errors, which included the location of the pump:

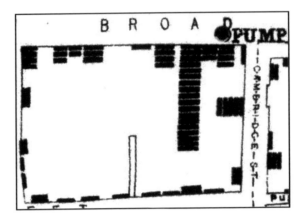

The text in this image is not important. It gives a gist of John Snow's second map

While essential components of geology existed beforehand in cartography, John Snow's guide was extremely remarkable. It was novel because of the way that he utilized cartographic techniques to portray as well as examine groups of geologically subordinate wonders. And because of this, John Snow is known to many as a pioneer in disease mapping, in which many of the concepts he established are still used today in conjunction with many other aspects of GIS by the **Centers for Disease Control and Prevention (CDC)**.

By the early 20th century, we saw the advancement of photozincography (also known as heliozincography). Photozincography gave the ability for maps to be split into layers. This meant that each layer could hold information only relevant to that specific layer, such as vegetation, trees, or waterways. It was mainly used for printing contours, since drawing these was a very labor-intensive task and thus made this technique extremely useful for cartographers. Having conduits, trees, or vegetation on independent layers implied that they could be chipped away at without alternate layers there to confound the artist, or to cause issues when, say, structures were obstructing something that should have been checked. This is also still used today; one such usage is when marking the location of electrical lines that are underground, or water pipes for houses:

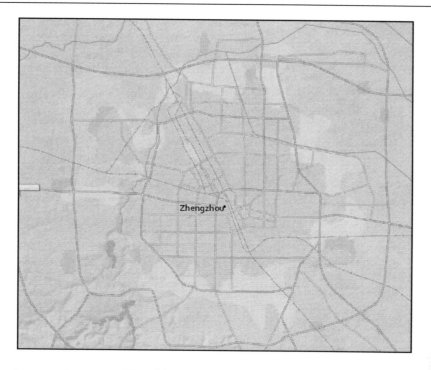

With photozincography, maps like this were initially drawn on glass plates but were later changed over to plastic film as there were numerous points of interest regarding plastic over glass. Plastic was lighter, required less space for capacity, was less fragile, and more. At the point when the greater part of the layers were done, they were joined into a solitary picture utilizing an extensive procedure camera. When color printing became available, the layers' conception was withal utilized for engendering separate plates for engendering each color.

The utilization of layers later became one of the main features of contemporary GIS, and the photographic process described is not considered to be a component of GIS itself as the maps were and are just images without any databases linked to them. Advancement of PC equipment that was impelled by atomic weapons prompted broadly useful PC mapping applications in the mid 1960s. In 1960, the world's first obvious operational GIS by the Federal Department of Forestry and Rural Development in Ottawa, Ontario, Canada was created.

This first obvious operational GIS was created by none other than Dr. Roger Tomlinson. This GIS was known as the **Canada Geographic Information System (CGIS)**, and it was utilized to store, break down, and control the information gathered for the Canada Land Inventory. The Canada Land Inventory was an administration push to decide the land capacity for provincial Canada by mapping data regarding the dirt, horticulture, amusement, untamed life, waterfowl, ranger service, and land use at a size of 1 to 50,000. Due to the scale and the amount of information that needed to be stored, a rating classification factor was created to permit easier and more effective analysis.

While there were other computer mapping applications at the time, CGIS made massive improvements as it provided capabilities for overlay, measurement, scanning, and digitizing the map data. It was also able to support a national coordinate system that spanned the entire continent with coded lines as arcs. This meant that it had a true embedded topology and it stored the attributes and locational information in separate files. The utilization of overlays in advancing the spatial investigation of focalized geographic information is the motivation behind Tomlinson turning out to be known as the "father of GIS".

In 1964, Howard T. Fisher shaped the Laboratory for Computer Graphics and Spatial Analysis at the Harvard Graduate School of Design (LCGSA 1965 – 1991), where a large number of essential hypothetical ideas in spatial information to be handled were produced. By the 1970s, seminal software code and systems were distributed by the LCGSA. These systems were SYMAP, GRID, and ODYSSEY; not only did these systems serve as sources for subsequent commercial development, but they themselves were distributed to colleges, research centers, and business conglomerates worldwide.

MOSS and GRASS GIS were two public GIS systems that were in development by the late 1970s. Roughly a few years later, in the early 1980s, new commercial vendors for GIS software emerged. Those commercial vendors were the Environmental Systems Research Institute, CARIS, MapInfo Corporation, ERDAS, and M&S Computing, along with Bentley Systems Incorporated for CAD. These sellers were fruitful in having the capacity to fuse numerous new highlights and ways to deal with GIS programming, for example, consolidating the original ways to deal with the partition of spatial and characteristic data with second-age ways to deal with sorting out trait information into database structures and additionally fusing CGIS highlights.

The first well-known work area GIS item that was discharged for the DOS OS was known as the Mapping Display and Analysis System, and was released to the public in 1986. In 1990, MIDAS was ported to the Microsoft Windows platform and was renamed to MapInfo for Windows during that process. This marked the process of moving GIS from the research sector over into the business sector.

One critical note to include is that CGIS kept going great into the 1990s and had fabricated a substantial advanced land asset database in Canada. CGIS was created as a centralized server-based framework for the government as a commonplace asset for arranging and administration programming. Along these lines, it had the capacity to do mainland wide investigation of complex datasets, however, CGIS was never made accessible in the business market sphere.

At the turn of the 20th century, users were beginning to explore GIS data over the internet. This called for data and transfer standardization. All of this was caused by the rapid growth in various systems and, as such, showcased the flaw that there were many different systems that used very few similar methods or data formats and needed to be consolidated.

As of late, there is an ever-growing number of open source GIS packages that run on a range of operating systems and software that are very easily customized to perform specific tasks. Research institutes and hobbyists are making mapping applications and geospatial data readily available via the internet.

GIS techniques and technologies

As stated in the previous section, GIS technologies heavily utilize digital information. There are quite a few different digital data formulation methods that are used. The most common method of data formulation, however, is digitization, for obvious reasons. Let's take a quick step back and define digitization. Digitization is where you have a physical copy of a map or survey data and transfer it into a digital medium by means of CAD or similar programs that have georeferencing capabilities. With the abundance of orthorectified imagery devices such as satellites, aircraft, Helikites, and UAVs, heads-up digitizing is becoming the go-to resource by which geographic data is extricated.

Heads-up digitizing is copying via tracing geographic data directly on top of aerial imagery. Heads-down digitizing is the process of tracing the geographic form onto a separate digitizing tablet, and is the more traditional method.

GIS can reference any variable that can be located spatially and temporally. Areas or degrees in Earth spacetime might be recorded as dates and times of event with the x, y, and z facilitates speaking to longitude, scope, and height. These GIS directions may speak to other information for measured frameworks of temporospatial reference. These GIS coordinates may represent other data for quantified systems of temporospatial reference. Some examples of temporospatial references include film frame number, stream gauge station, highway mile markers, surveyor benchmarks, building addresses, entrance gates, street intersections, water depth sounding, and POS or CAD origin or units.

Temporospatial data recorded units that are applied can vary widely; this includes using the exact same data, and because of this, all Earth-based spatial-temporal location references are relatable to one another. This makes it so that, ultimately, all of these references are able to represent a real physical location or extent in spacetime.

GIS data represents real objects with digital data determining the mix. That data includes objects such as roads, land use, elevation, trees, waterways, highways, and so much more. These real objects are generally divided into two distinct abstractions: discrete objects and continuous fields. Discrete objects are those such as houses, and continuous fields are things such as rainfall amount and evaluations. There are two broad methods that are used to store data in a GIS for both kinds of abstractions mapping references that have become a tradition: raster images and vectors. Points, lines, and polygons are typically used to map location attribute references.

There is a new hybrid method for storing data that is currently being used, which is able to combine three-dimensional points with RGB information at each point. This is able to return a 3D colorized image. GIS thematic maps are becoming much more realistically descriptive in what they are able to show or determine.

There are some very popular GIS file formats that are used by different software applications, such as the following:

- Shapefiles
- Geopackage
- World file
- AutoCAD DXF
- Cartesian coordinate system
- ADRG
- Binary files such as BSQ or BIP
- DRG
- ECRG
- GeoTiff
- JPEG2000
- RAW

Ways to capture GIS

Capturing GIS data consumes most available time for those that are practitioners of GIS. As such, there are a variety of methods used to enter data into a GIS where it is stored in a digital format. All existing data that has been printed on paper or PET film is able to be digitized or scanned to produce digital data. This would be a good time to define what a digitizer is and does.

A manual digitizer is a modified graphics tablet that uses a special magnetic pen, stylus, or puck that delivers information into a computer to create a digital map. These are rather expensive, however, they are very useful for GIS digitization (http://www.digitizerzone. com/calcomp-db6.html):

Digitizers can produce vector data as operator trace points, lines, and polygonal boundaries from a map. A scanner is able to scan the results into raster data, which needs to be further processed to produce vector data:

https://largeformatscanners.com/large-format-technical-scanners.htm

Using survey instruments and a technique called coordinate geometry, the data can be directly entered into a GIS. GPS (global positioning systems) positions can also be collected and imported into GIS software. The current popular approach to data collection allows for field computers to edit live data via wireless connections or offline editing sessions.

The higher availability of lower-cost mapping-grade GIS with the ability of to-the-decimeter accuracy in real time enhances the ability to use field computers to edit the live data as well as positions collected by laser rangefinders. The advantage of using this technique is that it eliminates most of the postprocessing, importation, and updating of the data in the office after fieldwork.

More and more new technologies are being developed that allow users to create maps and conduct analysis in the field directly, which makes projects and mapping more efficient and accurate. Remote sensor data is an important if not critical role in data collection, which consists of sensors attached to a platform. These sensors include cameras, digital scanners, and lidar, and the platforms usually consist of aircraft and satellites.

In the mid 1990s, England created a kite and balloon hybrid called HeliKites. They pioneered the use of compact digital cameras as geoinformation systems for aerial GIS data collection. Aircraft measurement software is accurate to 0.4 mm and is able to link the photographs with the measurements to the ground. The advantage of using HeliKites is that they can be used over towns, railways, and roads, where UAVs (unmanned aerial vehicles) are banned from usage. Miniature UAVs such as drones have recently been used for aerial data collection. Most digital data is collected from aerial photographs currently.

There are soft copy workstations that are used to digitize features from stereo pairs of digital photographs. The stereo pairs of digital photographs allow for data to be captured in both two and three dimensions. Elevation is measured using principles of photogrammetry. If analog aerial photos are used, they must be scanned before they can be entered into a soft copy workstation, however, if a high-quality digital camera is used, then this step can be skipped.

Remote sensing from satellites is another important source used for spatial data. Satellites use different sensor packages to measure the reflectance from parts of the electromagnetic spectrum and/or radio waves. Remote sensing from satellites collects raster data that is further processed with different frequency bands; this allows for better identification of objects and areas of interest.

No matter the source of captured data, it is important to consider if the data is captured with relative or absolute accuracy. Choosing between relative or absolute accuracy influences how the information is interpreted and the direct cost to capture the data.

After the data has been entered into a GIS, the data usually requires editing. The editing ensures that errors can be removed or designates which portions of the data need to be further processed. Scanned maps may have blemishes on the source map that may need to be removed from the raster image. Vector data has to be made topologically correct before usage with advanced analysis.

Converting from raster to vector

Data restored by GIS software can be converted into different formats. GIS can convert satellite image maps into vector structures. This is done by generating lines around cells within the same classifications. They can also determine the cell spatial relationships, such as adjacency and inclusion.

Image processing can do much more advanced data processing. This technique was developed in the 1960s by NASA, and was further enhanced by the private sector. They can do two-dimensional Fourier transforms, contrast enhancements, false color rendering, and a plethora of other techniques. Since digital data is stored and collected in different ways, the data sources tend to not be compatible with one another. To solve this compatibility problem, software built upon GIS technologies must be able to convert geographic data from one to the other. GIS are able to do this because they employ implicit assumptions behind different ontologies and classifications that require heavy analysis. Object ontologies have become much more prominent as a consequence of **object-oriented programming** (OOP), which makes it more compatible with game development and sustained work by Barry Smith and his coworkers.

Projections and coordinate systems

The Earth can be represented by various models, and all of them provide a different coordinate set for every point on the surface of the Earth. The simplest model assumes that the Earth is a perfect sphere, although we know it isn't. And as more measurements of the Earth have been accumulated, consequently, the models of Earth have become extremely sophisticated and accurate. There are models that have different data that apply to different areas of the Earth, which provides increased accuracy. NAD83 is a US measurement, and WGS84 (World Geodetic System) is for worldwide measurements.

There are clear but very minor differences between NAD83 and WGS84, besides one being worldwide and the other being US-based. WGS84 uses the WGS84 ellipsoid and has an error margin of less than 2 cm from the center of mass, whereas the NAD83 uses the Geodetic Reference System (GRS80) ellipsoid with an offset of about two meters. NAD83 uses points over the Northern American plate that do not change, and WGS84 uses points with respect to the average of stations all over the world and are not fixed. NAD83 has not changed since its inception; WGS84 has been revised to use a deviation of 105 m to +85 by the new EGM96 geoid. WGS84 is used by the US DOD (Department of Defense), and NAD83 is used by many other agencies within governments.

Although WGS84 and NAD83 have different parameters, the results have negligible effects during surveys. For example, the semi-minor axis has a difference of 0.00010482 between WGS84 and NAD83, and the inverse of flattening has a difference of 0.000001462 between the two. To better showcase this, let's look at a comparison of the US map from the results of WGS84 and NAD83:

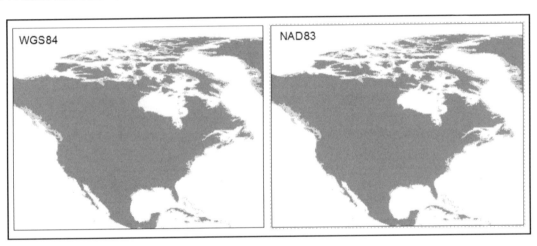

Spatial analysis with GIS

Spatial analysis allows us to better understand spatial relationships and patterns, which in turn allows us to better understand our world. Because of this, we are able to map where things are, how they relate to one another, what it all means for the environment, and actions to take to reverse any adverse effects we may cause. We are also able to find optimum routes, select sites for a plethora of different building projects, advanced predictive modeling, and so much more.

We can use the predictive modeling aspect to see how a forest fire would spread based on vegetation, dryness of the particular region, and wind. Not only that, but we could use it to find the optimal location for a store to be built that would likely attract the most customers.

Spatial analysis with GIS is a rapidly changing field. GIS packages are getting increasing amounts of analytical tools, which includes standard built-in libraries as well as optional toolsets and add-ons. Original software suppliers have provided these in many instances, however, third parties have been providing and developing these as well in increasing amounts. Many products offer SDKs (software development kits) that are compatible with specific programming languages, scripting capabilities, and the ability to develop custom analytical tools.

The website Geospatial Analysis (`http://www.spatialanalysisonline.com/`) and the associated book written by Michael J de Smith, Michael F Goodchild, and Paul A Longley are able to provide a fairly comprehensive guide on the subject matter. The massive increase in availability has created a new dimension to business and spatial intelligence to be able to make the geographic and social network data available to everyone. Geospatial intelligence, which is commonly referred to as GIS spatial analysis, has become a key element in security in the real world.

Data analysis with GIS

When trying to relate wetland maps to rainfall amounts recorded at different points, it can be difficult to do so, especially in places such as airports, schools, and television stations. A GIS can be used to visualize two-dimensional and three-dimensional characteristics of the Earth's surface. This also includes the atmosphere and subsurface from informational points as well. GIS can quickly generate map data from contour lines that have the ability to give the indications of differing amounts of precipitation. This type of map is called a rainfall contour map.

Many methods are able to estimate the characteristics of surfaces from limited point measurements and require a high level of sophistication to do so accurately. Two-dimensional contour maps that are created from the surface modeling precipitation points can be overlaid with any other map in GIS covering the same areas. This derived map is able to provide additional information; in this case, this would be the potential viability of water power as a renewable energy source. GIS can be used to compare many other renewable energy resource viability options for any geographic region.

Additionally, from a series of three-dimensional points, elevation contours can be generated from slope analysis, which would make it to easily define watershed locations by computing all the areas uphill from any point of interest. An expected line connecting the lowest points of successive cross sections along the course of a valley or river can be computed from elevation data as well.

From all of this, we are able to ascertain that there are five main steps in the data analysis process:

1. Framing the question
2. Exploring and preparing the data
3. Choosing the methods of analysis and the tools
4. Performing the analysis
5. Examining and refining the results

Framing the question: It is a good idea to frame the question to make the subsequent steps easier to go through, for example, frame the question in a manner that helps determine which GIS tools and methods will be used for analysis.

Exploring the data: This step is known to be the most time-consuming, and you aren't guaranteed to have all the data needed for the analysis. It is a good idea to know the data format that will be used, how current that data is, the scale and detail of the data, the coordinate system used, whether the data uses any geometry work with the analysis, whether the data has the attributes needed, and whether the data has any access or usage constraints.

Preparing the data: During this step, the data format to use will be extremely important to know as it will determine which set of tools will need to be used. Make sure the data is organized, the data is readily extractable, and there are no errors that occur when using the data in the tools that will be used.

Choosing the methods of analysis and the tools to be used: The methods and tools should be readily and easily defined by the question framed. Generally, the question should have a direct one-to-one for the methods and tools, and having a simple diagram for the analysis is considered good practice. A simple example is provided in the following image:

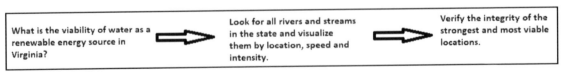

Performing the analysis: Since diagramming is considered good practice, all that needs to be done here is to follow the tasks in sequence. The more complex the analysis, the more it may be necessary to create a model with ModelBuilder to automate the process, which will make it easier to change a parameter and run the model again for different scenarios.

Examining and refining the results: This step is just to look at the results and see if there are additional parameters missed in the original question and add some tweaks to better fit the original vision of the question.

For a more detailed look, along with some tutorials on the steps in the data analysis process, visit `http://www.bcps.org/offices/lis/researchcourse/data_process.html`.

GIS modeling

GIS are able to recognize the spatial relationships that exist within stored spatial data as well as analyze said data. This allows for complex spatial modeling to be performed, studying the relationship between the properties of geometric forms that remain invariant, including adjacency, containment, and proximity. We can use this information to more accurately model and analyze the data.

Geometric networks

All of this leads us to geometric networks. Geometric networks are linear networks of objects that can be used to represent interconnected features and perform spatial analysis on them. Geometric networks are composed of edges that are connected at junction points. This is extremely similar to graph theory, which is heavily used in mathematics and computer science:

As we can see from the screenshot, networks can have weight and flow assigned to the edges, which are used to represent various connected features more accurately. The general use case for geometric networks is to model road networks and public utilities such as electric and water networks. They are also used to plan for transportation networks, infrastructure modeling, and hydrological modeling.

Hydrological modeling

Hydrological models in GIS provide spatial elements and analysis with variables such as slope, aspect, and catchment area. This includes terrain analysis, as it is fundamental to hydrology since water always flows down a slope. Slope and aspect can be used to determine the direction of a surface runoff and flow accumulation for streams, rivers, and lakes.

Areas of divergent flow also gives a clearer indication of boundaries regarding catchment. As flow direction and accumulation matrixes are created, queries can be performed to show dispersal areas. This allows for more details to be added to the model. This would be things such as roughness, vegetation types, soil types, evapotranspiration rates, and surface flow. All of this means that hydrological modeling is perfect for usage with environmental contamination research.

Cartographic modeling

Dana Tomlin coined the term "cartographic modeling" in his PhD dissertation in 1983, and he later used it in the title of his book *Geographic Information Systems and Cartographic Modeling*, which was published in 1990.

Cartographic modeling is the process wherein thematic layers of the same area are produced, processed, and analyzed. It should be noted that Tomlin used raster layers, however, the overlay method can be used in most general situations. Operations on map layers are able to then be combined with the usage of algorithms to be incorporated into simulations or optimization models.

Map overlays

Map overlay is the combination of several spatial datasets to create a new vector output dataset. You can visualize this by stacking several maps of the same area. Another way to visualize this is to think of the Venn diagram overlay used in mathematics. There are three types of overlays – union, symmetric difference, and intersect overlay – that are used for different reasons, which will not discussed here as they fall outside the scope of this book:

1. Union overlay is to combine geographic features and attribute tables of both inputs and output it to a single output
2. Intersect overlay is to define the area where both inputs overlap and retains a set of attribute fields for each

3. Symmetric difference overlay is to define the output area that includes the total area of both inputs EXCEPT for the overlapping area

Data extraction in GIS is very similar to a vector overlay with the ability to be used in either vector or raster data analysis. Instead of combining properties and features of both datasets, extracting the data can involve using a clip or mask to extract certain features of one dataset that are relevant to the other dataset.

Raster data analysis uses local operation on multiple raster datasets or map algebra. Map algebra has a function that combines the values of each raster's matrix and can be coupled with another function that can weigh some inputs higher than others through an index model that reflects the influence of various factors from within a geographic phenomenon.

Statistics used with GIS

Statistics is heavily used in GIS, and there is a special branch of statistics that deals with field data specifically. This special branch of statistics uses spatial data with a continuous index. It is able to provide methods to model spatial correlation and predict values at arbitrary locations, which is also known as interpolation.

When geographic phenomena are measured, the observation methods can dictate the accuracy of any analysis. There are limits caused by the nature of some data, where there is a constant or dynamic degree of precision that is always lost in measurement. This loss of precision is determined by the scale and distribution of the data collection.

When determining the statistical relevance of any analysis, the average has to be determined so that the points outside of any measurement can be included to their predicted behavior. Applied statistics and data collection methods have a limitation to predicting the behavior of particles, points, and locations, which causes them to not be directly measurable.

Interpolation is where a surface is created by raster datasets through the input of data collection at a certain number of sample points. There are, however, several different forms of interpolation, and each of them treats data differently, which is dependent on the properties of the dataset. When interpolation methods are compared, several points need to be considered. The first is whether or not that data source will change and whether exact or approximate data collection will be used. The next is whether a method is subjective, which essentially means whether human interpretation or objective interpretation methods will be used. Next is the nature of transitions between the points: are they gradual or abrupt? Finally, checking to see whether a method is local or global.

A global method utilizes the entire dataset to form the model, and a local method uses an algorithm to repeat for a small section of terrain. Interpolation is utilized as the fundamental technique for estimation because of the spatial autocorrelation rule, which says that information gathered at any position will have comparability to or impact over those areas inside its prompt region.

The mathematical methods to produce interpolative data are as follows:

- Digital elevation models
- Triangulated irregular networks
- Edge finding algorithms
- Thiessen polygons
- Fourier analysis
- Weighted moving averages
- Inverse distance weighting
- Kriging
- Spline
- Trend surface analysis

Geocoding

Geocoding is interjecting the x and y arrange spatial areas. These can be from road addresses or some other spatially referenced information, for example, ZIP codes, divide, and address areas. A reference topic is required to geocode singular locations, for example, a street centerline document with address ranges.

The individual address areas have verifiably been added, or assessed, by inspecting the address that goes along a street section. These are generally given in a table or database. The product will then place a spot around where that address has a place along the section of centerline. Geocoding can likewise be connected against genuine bundle information.

Reverse geocoding

Reverse geocoding is the way toward restoring an expected road address number, as it identifies with a given facilitate. You can think about this like an invert telephone number look-into table. Also, similar to reverse phone look-into tables, switch geocoding does not return real road addresses, just the gauge of what ought to be there in light of a foreordained range. Combined with GIS, multi-criteria choice examination techniques bolster leaders in breaking down an arrangement of option spatial arrangements. MCDA utilizes choice tenets to total the criteria, which enables the elective answers to be positioned or organized. GIS MCDA may diminish expenses and time engaged with recognizing potential reclamation destinations.

Open Geospatial Consortium Standards

The **Open Geospatial Consortium (OGC)** is a non-profit association that was established in 1994 and has more than 384 organizations, colleges, government offices, and individuals taking part to grow freely accessible geoprocessing particulars.

OpenGIS Specifications have conventions and interfaces characterized to help arrangements that empower the web, remote, area administrations, tech engineers, and standard IT to make complex spatial data and administrations available and valuable for a heap of utilization composes.

Web Map Services and Web Feature Services are incorporated into the OGC conventions. Any product items that consent to OGC's OpenGIS particulars are known as Compliant Products, and when an item has been tried and affirmed by the OGC testing program, it is consequently enlisted as consistent on the open geospatial database.

The procedure by which to wind up "OGC guaranteed" has five stages:

- Go to the testing website and select the standard for the product desired
- Go to the OGC Online Certification system and provide the information about the product, testing account, and standard for certification desired

- OGC will review and contact regarding the licensing fee and a new or revised trademark license agreement
- Receive the certificate, and the OGC compliance logos are then open for usage
- Product will then appear as certified in the OGC implementing database

Full information can be found at the official website at `http://www.opengeospatial.org/compliance/getCertified`:

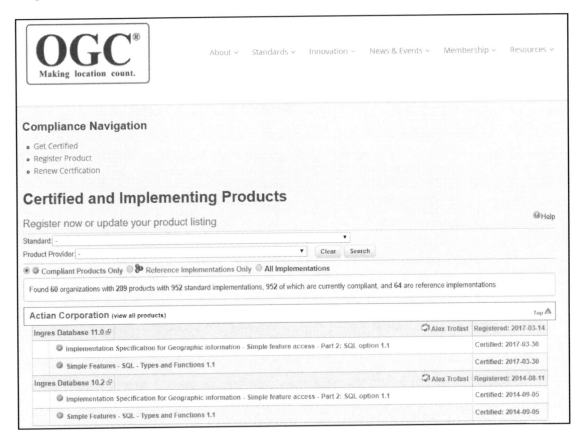

Note that consistence tests are not accessible for all determinations. Designers can enroll their items as actualizing draft or endorsed particulars, despite the fact that OGC maintains whatever authority is needed to audit and check every section.

Web mapping

As of late, numerous allowed to utilize and effectively available exclusive mapping programming, for example, Google Maps, Bing Maps, Apple Maps and Baidu Maps what's more, there is additionally some free and open source options like OpenStreetMap, GMap.NET, Wikimapia, RMaps, and uebermaps. These administrations give the free to a lot of GIS injected mapping information.

A significant number of them offer an API (application programming interface) that take into account clients to make custom applications or broaden the current application. These libraries or systems tend to offer road outline, satellite symbolism, flying symbolism, geocoding, georeferencing, geofencing, seeks, and directing usefulness. Crowdsourcing geodata in ventures such as web mapping has been found to make a communitarian task to make free and editable maps of the world for all that need to utilize that particular application or informational index.

GIS and adding dimension of time

The state of the Earth, this is the subsurface, environment and surface can be broken down by encouraging satellite information into GIS programming. GIS have enabled specialists to utilize the innovation to investigate the varieties of the Earth's procedures over days, months, years, and even decades. Vegetation wellbeing changes through the developing season can be reenacted to decide when a dry season would have the most serious effect in any given district. The outcomes can give a harsh measure of the soundness of the plants in a recreated district. Simply utilizing two factors and estimating them after some time enables analysts to decide separations in the decay of precipitation and the outcomes on the locale's vegetation.

The accessibility of advanced data with both local and worldwide scales empowers GIS innovation to make such examinations. Satellite sensors deliver pictures of a specific area of the Earth twice every day. MODIS (Moderate Resolution Imaging Spectroradiometer) and AVHRR (advanced very-high-resolution radiometer) are two of numerous sensor frameworks utilized for examination of the Earth's surface. These sensor frameworks can recognize the measures of vitality reflected from the Earth's surface crosswise over different groups of the recurrence range for territories up to one square kilometer.

Not exclusively is time being incorporated into ecological examinations with GIS, however, the capacity to track and model the advancement of people and creatures all through their everyday schedules is being investigated. This can be seen with the Google and Facebook area benefits that track a man for the duration of the day for a considerable length of time, months, or even a very long time after use. This compose information creation and control could never have been conceivable without GIS and the extraordinary type of insights utilized. Organizers can, likewise, test strategy choices by utilizing spatial choice emotional supportive network by utilizing models to extend the information encased inside a GIS forward in time.

Semantics

The World Wide Web Consortium's Semantic Web ended up being amazingly helpful for incorporating information issues in data frameworks through devices and advances that have been developing. These apparatuses and innovations have been proposed as methods for interoperability and information reuse among different GIS-based applications and take into consideration new examination mechanics.

A few arrangements of ideas and classes of this space to indicate formal and machine-clear particulars of their ideas and connections have been made. This takes into account GIS to center around the information rather than the language structure or structure of the information. Easier ontologies alongside semantic metadata measures have been recommended by the W3C Geo Incubator Group, particularly to speak to geospatial information on the web. One such case is GeoSPARQL, which is a Geographic Query dialect for **Resource Description Framework (RDF)** Data, in which there are different advancements that are based on RDF and give dialect to characterizing the real structure, for example, **Web Ontology Language (OWL)** and **Simple Knowledge Organization System (SKOS)**.

GeoSPARQL was produced by the **Open Geospatial Consortium (OGC)** and has been bolstered by numerous people in the field and not restricted to the Ordinance Survey, United States Geological Survey, Natural Resources Canada, Industrial Research Organization, and Austrialia's Commonwealth Scientific. GeoSPARQL gives OGC literals, for example, **Geography Markup Languague (GML)** and WTK (surely understood content) and simple highlights, for example, RCC8 (locale association analytics) and DE-9IM (Dimensionally Extended nine-crossing point demonstrate) give topological relationship and subjective thinking and, in addition, SPARQL expansion capacities and **Rule Interchange Format (RIF)** center derivation rules for questioning change and elucidation.

Later research comes about here, and can be found at the International Conference on Geospatial Semantics web workshop and International Semantic Web Conference.

The implications of GIS in society

GIS is ending up, to a great degree, well-known with basic leadership as of late, and researchers have started to look profoundly into the social and political ramifications of GIS. Similarly, as with any frame and information accumulation and examination, GIS is defenseless to be abused to misshape reality for political and individualistic pick up. The generation, circulation, use, and portrayal of geographic data has been contended to be generally identified with the social setting, and furthermore holds the potential for expanded native doubt in the administration.

Different points that are investigated intensely are regarding potential copyright infringement, oversight, and protection. Many in the field are more hopeful, and they trust that the social approach that many will adopt is to strategize GIS appropriation as an instrument for open cooperation.

GIS in the real world

Not only can GIS be used in the academic sector, but it can also be used in the real world very effectively. We have seen the rise of GPS apps, which have largely replaced traditional maps, apps that know your exact location, apps that can find a lost device or child, and so much more. By taking all of the topographical and statistical data that can be obtained, almost every sector in modern life has been or can be utilized for GIS data.

We can really see this from historical events; let's use the bubonic plague as an example. Unlike those in the past, we are armed with hindsight that is 20/20; we know that it was rats that spread the disease. Let's say we had all of the data that showcased the movement and travel information of the rats, which we could then have used to study their patterns and have a much more accurate description of where the plague started and how it traveled.

It doesn't stop there, since that is more on the academic approach as well. Let's say we want to track our own daily patterns within the last five years. We can use location data along with GIS to accurately depict our daily routine. We can move forward and also think about how we can use GIS to track our internet usage by creating a GIS specific for IP addresses that showcases how frequently and infrequently websites are accessed.

Then, there are video games; we can apply GIS to video games in a multitude of ways, from recreating terrain used in historic battle locations from all around the world, to creating a completely alien world from mixing GIS data from various planets and moons. But we could also use GIS to augment the reality around us by injecting GIS data into the camera to transform or recognize similar data from which it reads in real time.

GIS in education

At the turn of the 20th century, GIS was starting to be recognized as a tool for use in the classroom. GIS used in education has the benefit of being focused on the development of spatial thinking. The downside is that there is little statistical data to show the scope of the usage of GIS around the world, although countries that specifically have a curriculum that mentions GIS have expanded faster.

GIS in local governments

GIS has proven to be an organization-wide enterprise, and a highly enduring technology that continues to adapt how the local government operates on many tasks. Many, if not all, governmental agencies have adopted GIS technology as a method to better manage and improve upon many of their organizations, such as:

- Public Safety operations such as Emergency Operations Centers, Fire Prevention, Police and Sheriff mobile technology and dispatch, and mapping weather risks
- Parks and Recreation departments and their functions in asset inventory, land conservation, land management, and cemetery management
- Public Works and Utilities, tracking water and storm water drainage, electrical assets, engineering projects, and public transportation assets and trends
- Fiber Network Management for interdepartmental network assets
- School analytical and demographic data, asset management, and improvement/expansion planning
- Public Administration for election data, property records, and zoning/management

The Open Data Initiative has pushed the local government to take advantage of the technology and also share their own data with their requirements to fit the Open Data and Open Government model of transparency. Because of Open Data, local government organizations can implement their online portals which allow citizens to view and utilize this information. This push for open data from within and outside of government organizations has been a huge driving force for local government GIS tech spending and database management.

GIS and augmented reality

As discussed in the previous section, the application of GIS with augmented reality is only really hampered by your imagination, especially when you consider that there are tons of data types that you can utilize from GIS data. So, in the next section, we will go over and think of ways we can apply GIS to augmented reality applications and games.

Applications of GIS

As Richie Carmichael of the Esri Applications Prototype Lab said to Keith Mann in an online article (`http://www.esri.com/news/arcuser/0311/augmented-reality-and-gis.html`):

> *"Imagine that you could point the camera on your phone at the ground and see the location and orientation of water pipes and electric cables buried under the ground because your AR app is cross-referencing the GIS system with your location and giving you a kind of x-ray vision so that you can visualize the infrastructure that is underneath you."*

This mindset has been reflected by many companies such as Google, Tencent, Microsoft, Facebook, Twitter, Apple, and many more. China's Tencent has done quite a few things with augmented reality and GIS. I think it is very worthwhile to go over some of the things China have done with AR and GIS.

China does not use Google's services whatsoever and had to create their own search engine, which is called Baidu. This also means that they had to make mapping software which fully utilizes GIS. They created Baidu Maps, which works just like Bing Maps and Google Maps, however, they have added a slight twist to it. You can add a separate package for it that allows it to be easily used or integrated into AR applications.

By wearing smartglasses, it will project the map in front of you with the number of steps you have walked, and a first-person overlay of where you need to go to get to your destination.

They have also heavily integrated their social media platforms, QQ and Wechat, to work with their map software, which leads me to Wechat's share real-time location function. It displays where you are and the location of the person you are trying to meet in real time, and updates with every step you take.

Google of course has Google Maps, which obviously works very similarly to Baidu Maps and Bing Maps. This leaves Apple Maps, which was the first to heavily integrate AI for auditory augmentation into their map service. AutoCAD and Blender are two programs that have the ability to read and manipulate GIS data. They can import shapefiles and create a 3D representation of the terrain, or export this as a specified file format. In AutoCAD's case, it can export the data to XML, which can then be used to extract specific information that is wanted, such as population densities, or things along those lines.

AuGeo was made by Esri and it is a form of open source programming. This product enables you to control, download, and see information straightforwardly on a cell phone in a first-person view. AuGeo consolidates enlarged reality with GIS and shows highlighted information upon a live camera feed so that you can investigate your GIS information.

Augview, made by Augview Limited, is both a versatile GIS, enabling clients to see and alter their benefit information from the field, and an increased reality application, enabling clients to imagine underground protests they wouldn't normally observe. These are just a couple of players in the immense pool of organizations and applications that have been created to use, see, and/or control GIS information. Before we proceed, we should investigate a few applications that exploit GIS and augmented reality.

EyeMaps enables you to get data on a chosen dialect. Simply utilize camera mode to get thoughts about world around you. It immediately gives you names of mountains, urban communities, towns, exhibition halls, and much more. Take after connections to Wikipedia to get more data. Watch and offer your photographs on a 3D outline. This current application's primary highlights are making a 3D guide of your general surroundings while giving you data checks on it.

Vortex Planetarium is an excellent and simple application about everything in the sky. Huge amounts of information exists, including everything of the night sky substance, a large number of stars, groups of stars, messier articles, Caldwell items, and significantly more. This present application's fundamental highlights are exceedingly configurable substances. Set the straightforwardness of group of stars workmanship or tap the number of stars you wish to find in the night sky.

Plane Finder lets you see all air activity around the globe continuously. Interim the application gives you profoundly redid substance to set everything for your requirements. With Augmented Reality, you can recognize planes overhead with your gadget camera. The application additionally permits to set warnings when a plane shows up in the sky above you. This present application's fundamental highlights are that it works by getting ongoing ADS-B signals. This innovation is speedier than a customary radar!

iOnRoad enables you to make a highly practical gadget from your cell phone. It offers help to you with GPS, activity checking, video and picture catching, and considerably more. This present application's principal highlights are that it utilizes your gadget's local camera, GPS, and sensors to recognize vehicles before you, preparing drivers when they are in danger.

Dino around my work area AR amusement allows you to attempt to pet a virtual dinosaur. Inquisitive and adorable looking dinosaurs from ages past will meander around your work area. You may play with it by hand, or by tapping it in plain view of the screen. You may even sustain it. Be that as it may, whatever you do – remember, it has a voracious temper! This current application's principal highlights are that it enables you to play and find out about the ancient universe of dinosaurs.

The EmotionsAR application is for the individuals who saw vivified photographs in Harry Potter and constantly needed one for themselves. EmotionsAR furnishes you with a selective shot that enables you to make the photo come alive. What it would be? A short-energized photograph, or a long video story? That's for you to decide. This present application's principle highlights are that you can create your own particular photographs with AR video content!

Crayola Color Alive enables you to breathe life into your shading illustrations with vivid models that ascent up from the Crayola-lined pages. Spare your best characters to impart to your loved ones and utilize them whenever. This present application's principle highlights are that it has huge amounts of characters, enables you to print free pages, or obtained packs, at that point shading them and breathing life into them.

Gaming and GIS

Gaming and GIS is a very interesting topic, and there are a multitude of ways to incorporate this idea with AR since AR has different ways of being implemented. To really showcase a prime example of incorporating GIS into games and applying a form of augmented reality, we need to look no further than the most well-known MMO of all time, World of Warcraft.

To set the stage, we first need to explain some of the features of World of Warcraft and what data modders have to work with. World of Warcraft has many different professions that you can do, and all of them require that you collect the materials necessary to craft the items. There are different types of cloth, ore, flowers, archeology spot locations, cooking recipes, and many different crafting recipes that can be found all throughout the world. And this is ignoring armor, weapons, randomly spawning rare mobs, and world boss locations that can be found through the world.

In order to incorporate GIS into World of Warcraft, people mapped the terrain of the world map or pulled the data from the data files in the game, mapped locations of everything that spawns all throughout the world, and abstracted them into different layers that correlate with what they reference. Then, they overlay them over the world map and attach them to the mini map to show where they are while playing the game with the mod enabled.

As you can see, augmented reality doesn't just apply to the real world, but also the fantasy world as well. This makes AR very versatile, especially when you can find ways to incorporate GIS into it. Next up, let's take a look at some pure AR games that focus on the real world. The primary game we will look at is GeoGuessr. GeoGuessr began as a little web application that gives you the test of speculating the areas of a progression of irregular Street View pictures. After you've made your guess, it uncovers the genuine area and honors focuses in view of how close you get.

The next game we will look at is Pursued. It is a sought-after shockingly fun Street View amusement game from Hungarian diversion designers Nemesys Games. The fundamental subject of the diversion is as per the following: "You've been taken all of a sudden. A companion is endeavoring to help you; however, you should make sense of where you are!" The point of the amusement is to guess the name of the city you take a gander at and type the name in the textbox as quickly as possible. In case you can't guess by the visual pieces of information in the Street View, you can move around by clicking in the Street View picture and utilize your '+' and '-' keys to zoom in and out.

Third on the rundown is Smarty Pins. Smarty Pins is a game created by Google Engineers. The point is to discover the response to an inquiry and stick point this area on the guide. For instance, you would get the inquiry "Where is the most seasoned British college?" and you would need to put a stick on Oxford. The main inquiries are normally situated in a player's nearby nation or are identified with extremely well-known places or individuals, however, as you advance, the playing board grows to whatever is left of the world and gets more challenging.

Guide Race is number four on the rundown. The thought behind it is to demonstrate to you a satellite photo of an area and four possible answers. The challenge is to choose the right answer at the earliest opportunity. In the event that you guess the wrong city, you'll get more opportunities to fathom it, which is terrible.

Number five is MapsTD. MapsTD is a pinnacle barrier game that utilizes Google Maps to create levels from any area over the world. Your undertaking is to safeguard your palace from assailants by deliberately putting and dealing with your guard towers. It's a truly standard pinnacle protection setup, yet the delight originates from doing it crosswise over true lanes and areas.

Number six on the rundown is Build. It is an impact of coordinated effort of Google and LEGO to exhibit potential outcomes of Google Chrome. It let clients build anything they can envision with virtual LEGO, put it on Google Maps, and offer their manifestations to the world. As the name suggests, it only works in Google Chrome.

Geo Guns is a tank shooting game and is number seven on our rundown. The diversion takes a full preferred standpoint of Google Maps' 45° (Bird's Eye) satellite view. It overlays a few tanks on the satellite picture. Your assignment is to crush the enemy tanks. You can browse various preset war zone areas for your tank battle, yet you can choose any area by entering an area on the highest point of the screen.

Find Street is a StreetView-based game and is number eight. It gives you a progression of irregular Street View scenes. Your assignment is to make sense of the area of each picture and pick the right test reply. As you can see, you can very easily utilize GIS, georeferencing, and AR in your games all at the same time, or by utilizing various aspects of each of these to create them.

The key things to keep in mind and remember are as follows:

- Map design and the player interactions with maps are an essential part of the undertaking of creating a video game.
- The game's appearance, graphics-wise, therefore sets its tone just as much as the control experience, insecurity, exploration, or plot do.
- In competitive titles, the map represents the playing field. Every corner, every little modification, is crucial, as the players take their positions based on that. Monitoring this positioning is a must for the winning team.
- In open map titles, the game experience often exceeds the information provided by the maps.

These items are critical for determining which approach best fits the idea and structure you want to implement.

Summary

In this chapter, we discussed the history of GIS, how GIS data is collected, how GIS data is used, GIS applications, GIS games, and how to incorporate GIS into augmented reality applications and games. There were many more interesting bits of information provided, such as the data formats and how they changed with time; we learned that GIS has many applications, both in the past and in the present for statistics and analysis, that will most likely continue to be used in the future here on Earth and on other planets, as we are starting to see with Mercury, Venus, Mars, and our Moon.

GIS is a broad field that has the ability to be applied in many different ways and for a variety of purposes, and in learning the basic fundamentals of GIS and its history, we can now apply that information to the games and applications we create. In the next chapter, we will learn about sensors and plugins with Unity.

Questions

1. The history of GIS began in the year 1970:

     A.) True
     B.) False

2. GIS stands for Geographic Information Strategy:

     A.) True
     B.) False

3. Christopher Picquet conducted the first known application of spatial analysis:

     A.) True
     B.) False

4. John Snow found an accurate source for the cholera outbreak in 1854:

     A.) True
     B.) False

5. John Snow is known to many as a pioneer of disease mapping:

     A.) True
     B.) False

6. GIS is used by the CDC today for disease mapping:

     A.) True
     B.) False

7. Heads-up digitizing is copying via tracing geographic data directly on top of aerial imagery:

     A.) True
     B.) False

8. Popular GIS file formats include Shapefiles, AudoCAD DXF, and GeoTiff:

    A.) True
    B.) False

9. GIS is not used in determining geographic locations when used in applications:

    A.) True
    B.) False

10. GIS is not used in any capacity for education:

    A.) True
    B.) False

3
Censored - Various Sensor Data and Plugins

I hope you'll excuse the cheeky pun in the title. In this chapter, we will discuss the various sensors that we can access through the various SDKs provided to us. This includes ARKit, Vuforia, ARCore, Swift API, and the Java API. Now, the reason we will be going with this route is because there are some things in the core APIs that are not exposed in the SDKs provided to Unity but that we can leverage using native plugins with wrapper calls in C#. To break this up, to be a little more succinct without going outside of the bounds of this book, I will not be teaching the syntax of the Java or Swift programming languages; there are already some fantastic books that have been written by other Packt authors that cover this material, such as *Beginning Swift* (`https://www.packtpub.com/application-development/beginning-swift`) and *Java Programming for Beginners* (`https://www.packtpub.com/application-development/java-programming-beginners`).

This chapter will be broken down into several main sections, as follows:

- Leveraging sensors with Plugins
- Writing Unity Plugins
- C# Language Plugin
- C++ Language Plugin
- Swift Language Plugin
- Objective-C Language Plugin
- Java Language Plugin

By breaking the chapter down into these distinct sections, we can make it much easier for you to find the specific section you want.

Project overview

We will create basic plugins in C#, C++, Swift, Objective-C, and Java. Each one will be an implementation of a basic mathematical return value. Writing the plugins in their native code should take no more than 10 minutes to complete for each native code snippet. You must have a working test in Unity.

Getting started

When dealing with AR Applications and games, there are bound to be prerequisites, and with this book this will be no different.

The following are the requirements for an Apple Mac computer:

- macOS 11
- Xcode 9
- Mono Framework **5.14.0**
- Unity 2017
- ARKit

It is suggested that you have a 2013 or later model Mac computer, as older versions do not support the Metal API for graphics.

When you install Unity on a Mac, it will install Visual Studio for Mac as well; the catch is it requires Mono Framework to run, so be sure to download and install everything.

Here are the requirements for a Windows computer:

- Windows 10
- 8 GB of RAM or more
- Unity
- ARCore
- JDK 8 or higher
- Visual Studio
- Android Studio

For more information, click on these links:

```
https://store.unity.com/
https://developer.apple.com/arkit/
http://www.mono-project.com/download/stable/#download-mac
https://www.visualstudio.com/
https://developer.Android.com/studio/
```

Sensors

First things first, we need to get a good grasp of what sensors are and what they can be used for, before we get into the various mini projects that will coincide with each of the SDKs we will be using. This list of sensors is by no means a complete list and are some of the most common ones that we can leverage in AR applications and games:

- Fingerprint Sensor
- Radiation Sensor
- Heart Rate Monitor
- Pedometer
- Air Humidity Sensor
- Thermometer
- Barometer
- Light Sensor
- Proximity Sensor
- Magnetometer
- Gyroscope
- Accelerometer
- Ambient Light Sensor
- Iris Scanner
- IR Blaster
- Touch Sensor
- Microphone
- Camera
- GNSS
- NFC
- Laser
- Air Gesture Sensor

- Signal Receiver
- LiFi
- Clock

In this section, we will describe what each of these sensors is and what they can be used for, besides their native functions.

Proximity Sensor: The proximity sensor can detect when the cellphone is within a certain range of objects and manipulate software or hardware to react in a certain way, once the sensor's trigger has been tripped. It is generally used to reduce the total amount of battery consumption by dimming the backlight of the cellphone when it reaches a certain range of the user's ear or pocket. Theoretical usage in AR games and applications requires a little bit of thinking outside the box. We know that a proximity sensor can't detect the difference between objects, so what we could do is detect whether there are multiple objects near the device and register an event based on that.

Gyroscope: The gyroscope is a sensor designed to read and output the direction of a cellphone or device with the sensor installed. It is generally used to power apps and detect the orientation of the device to determine whether the UI should be displayed in landscape or portrait mode. Theoretical usage in AR games and applications could be to use the device to act as a compass for traversing the game world.

Fingerprint scanner sensor: The fingerprint scanner sensor is a sensor designed to detect whether pressure has been added to a special plate and to read the input data from the plate.
It is generally used to add an additional layer of security over a login password. It is much more secure and harder to bypass than most standard passwords, even with AES encryption with salting.

Camera: The camera is itself a sensor. It is able to able to digitize waves of light and the electromagnetic radiation emitted so that a device can interpret the information and display it in a way that is understandable to the user. It is generally used to take pictures to store and retrieve.

Barometer: The barometer sensor is designed to detect changes in the atmospheric pressure, which in turn means it can effectively act as a means of forecasting the weather. It is generally used to determine the weather in the general vicinity where the user is located.

Thermometer: The thermometer sensor is a sensor used to detect changes in temperature and store/send that information to be displayed or acted upon. It is generally used to keep track of and measure the temperature of sensitive components in the device.

Accelerometer: The accelerometer is a sensor designed to detect the momentum of the device, and, by extension, detect the momentum of the user. It is generally used to determine the speed in which the user is travelling while in possession of the device.

Pedometer: The pedometer is a sensor that is designed to take the user's momentum within the confines of human speed limits and convert it into steps walked. It is generally used to calculate the user's daily step count and display it at a specific time for the user to review.

Touch sensor: The touch sensor is designed to detect when a user's finger touches the device's screen and return the position and length of time the finger was in that location. It is generally used to activate and manipulate all the basic and advanced usage for the device.

Microphone: The microphone is a sensor designed to detect sound waves and convert them into digital information that the device can understand and store. It is generally used to pick up the sound waves during a phone call and transmit that data to a connected device remotely.

Ambient light sensor: The ambient light sensor is designed to react to a variety of light conditions in such a way that it mimics how the human eyes would perceive and react to those different light scenarios. It is generally used for power saving by adjusting the backlight intensity levels (lighten or darken the screen), based on the lighting of the area around the device.

Iris Scanner sensor: The iris scanner sensor is designed to create high-resolution images of the eye. It is used mainly for security purposes. It is considered a form of biometric security, as it will only accept data from a specific eye for unlocking the device.

Air gesture sensor: The air gesture sensor is able to detect via infrared sensors — movements from hands in front of the device's screen. It is generally used to add basic control of the device without needing to use the touch screen, for example, activating the screen or applications.

Heart rate monitor sensor: The heart rate monitor sensor is a sensor designed to be able to track someone's heartbeat using a combination of algorithms, green LEDs, and the accelerometer to measure blood flow, and store this information. It is generally used to accurately measure your heartbeat during exercise.

Air Humidity Sensor: The air humidity sensor is a thermal conductivity sensor that utilizes aspects of the temperature sensor to be able to detect humidity.

Light sensor: There are many different types of light sensors that could be photoresistors, photodiodes, or even phototransistors. They are designed to detect whether there is light in a given area and, if so, how much light is available. A light sensor generally works in tandem with the ambient light sensor to give accurate light assessment for taking pictures.

Magnetometer: The magnetometer is a sensor designed for measuring magnetic forces. Magnetometers are generally used for treasure-finder apps.

IR Blaster sensor: The IR Blaster sensor is a sensor designed to emulate an infrared remote control. It is generally used to create a universal remote control app for a variety of devices.

GNSS (Global Navigation Satellite System): GNSS is a sensor designed to pick up signals from multiple satellites for better accuracy, availability, and redundant data collection. It is generally used to poll for a user's location in order to give more accurate results in a GPS app.

NFC (Near-Field Communication): NFC sensors are designed to be wireless data transferers for proximity-based communication. They are generally used for using services such as Apple Pay and Apple Wallet payments.

Signal receiver sensor: The signal receiver sensor is a sensor designed to receive radio waves and convert them into a digital form that the device can understand. It is generally used for telephone calls or for playing music from the radio.

LiFi sensor: LiFi sensors, also known as *Light Fidelity Sensors,* use **Light-emitting diodes (LEDs)** to transmit data. They are generally used for areas that cannot use Wi-Fi, such as power plants, to send and receive data.

Clock: The **Real-Time Clock** or **RTC** is designed to accurately keep track of the time. It is a clock that shows the exact time.

Leveraging sensors with plugins

As previously stated, we can access the information provided by any exposed piece of hardware and send that information to our applications and/or games we create within Unity. The catch is that if there isn't an implementation within Unity or the SDKs we are using for AR applications, we will need to create a plugin with a wrapper to access that sensor.

This is also heavily dependent on which devices we want to target and whether we want to target both iOS and Android-based devices without any implementations done for us. If so, then we need to create the plugin ourselves. We can't just write a plugin in C#, though; we would need native plugins to call upon these sensors to do our bidding. This means that we will need to utilize the Java and Swift languages for their respective operating systems. For Android, the native-level code would be Java or C++, and for iOS, the native-level code would be Swift, Objective-C, or C++.

It is extremely important that we first understand how the sensor values are returned to us from the JDK and Apple SDKs. The JDK breaks all of the sensors down into specific categories. The accelerometer, the gyroscope, and the pedometer are all in the motion sensors category; the temperature sensor is located within the environment sensors category.

There is an imperative distinction to be made between the categories that need to be fully understood. The environment sensors category returns a single sensor value for each sensor event; meanwhile, the motion sensors category will return a multi-dimensional array of each sensor event that occurs. With this tidbit of information out of the way, let's move on to the next section, where we will learn how to write and dissect basic plugins for Unity in C++, C#, Java, Swift, and Objective-C.

Writing unity plugins

The first thing we need to do is gain an understanding of what a plugin is for Unity before we can create and dissect a very simple plugin for Unity.

What is a plugin?

A *plugin* is a dll file that stores code written in a different programming language that is a base implementation of some event that needs to be executed or in the same language that gives the base implementation of core code that functions as a library or non-changeable event.

Now, this is a very simplistic definition, but we can do better by explaining what they can do for the developer, or a developer who wants to utilize code you have written. Plugins allow a developer to extend existing code without having to trudge through the source library by accessing methods and properties that are made public to them, which adds new features to the game engine that is not natively present, separates operating system-specific code, and they can reduce the size of an application.

For Unity specifically, plugins allow us to directly interface with native calls and use them as we wish in our application or games. Many developers tend to create plugins with native system calls to extend the render pipeline or for enhancing shaders.

It is important to note that there are two very distinct plugin types available to use in Unity. Those two types are **Native Plugins** and **Managed Plugins**. A very simplified explanation of the difference between native and managed plugins is that native plugins are for low-level calls, and managed plugins are an easy way to hide source code.

There is, however, a more nuanced differentiation between them than this old adage.

A managed plugin can and will easily hide source code from prying eyes when a developer wants to sell something in the asset store. It can also be used to include libraries and frameworks that are not otherwise readily available to Unity. For example, a developer could import the Entity Framework dll files into Unity and utilize the Entity Framework to create, manage, and handle database code with Unity. The final thing that a managed plugin can do is allow a developer to utilize some .NET languages and compilers that are not supported by Unity, such as F#, JScript, IronPython, ClosureCLR, or even Powershell. For example, a developer could create a plugin for Unity that allows for scripting in IronPython, or they could write game code using IronPython and import it as a plugin and use it without issues.

A native plugin, on the other hand, is profoundly more powerful. A native plugin normally consists of using Java, Swift, Objective-C, or C++ to access the direct hardware of their respective devices and provide functionality that a developer could otherwise not have access to within Unity. Let's say a developer is working with a device that connects to a smartphone that is not normally present in smartphones; in this case, we will go with the **BACtrack Mobile Pro** as our example.

The BACtrack Mobile pro is a police-grade breathalyzer that can check a user's blood alcohol content and send that information to a device via Bluetooth connections. This developer wants to make a drinking-style AR game, and they want to make the game harder, the higher the end user's BAC level is. This developer would need to use a native plugin to gain access to the BACtrack device's sensors' results.

Now that a firm understanding should have been gained from this explanation, we can finally start looking at the structure of a plugin for C++, Swift, C#, and Java. What we will do is create a very simple plugin that will simply add two numbers together. This is to keep things simple and allow for the flow of steps for the overall workflow to be much more easy to follow.

There is a list of file types that Unity will automatically recognize as plugins. It is very important that we familiarize ourselves with these file formats:

- .dll
- .winmd
- .so
- .JAR
- .aar
- .xex
- .def
- .suprx
- .prx
- .sprx
- .rpl
- .cpp
- .cc
- .c
- .h
- .jslib
- .jspre
- .bc
- .a
- .m
- .mm
- .swift
- .xib

Then there are also folder types that are treated as single plugins; they are as follows:

- .framework
- .bundle
- .plugin

With native plugins for Unity, you can run into C linkage issues that will cause a phenomenon called **Name Mangling**. Name mangling is also called *name decoration*, which is essentially a process that gives each function in a program a unique name; this is so that the linkers can separate common names in the language. The issue comes from the fact that there is no standard for this, and they typically don't work well with C compilers.

C# language plugin

Let's get started by creating our first plugin with C#:

1. We need to begin by opening Visual Studio and creating a new project. This new project type will be inside the **Windows Desktop** subfolder of **Visual C#** and will need to be a **Class Library (.NET Framework)**:

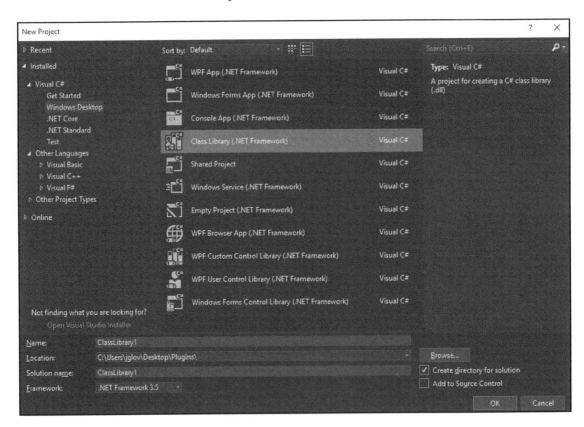

Project type

2. The project name will be `CSharpManagedPlugin`, and the Framework version will be `.NET Framework 3.5`. Select the **OK** button:

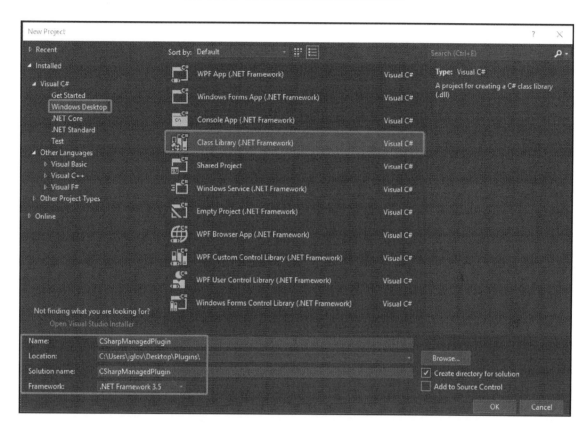

Project setup

 Making sure to change the Framework version to 3.5 is extremely important, as we need to make sure that Unity can utilize our plugin without experimental support.

3. Now that we have created our solution, we can change the class name from Class1 to Addition. Now, add an integer method called addify with the parameters of a and b, and then return a plus b. Your code should look as follows:

```
namespace CSharpManagedPlugin
{
    public class Addition
    {
        public int Addify(int a, int b)
        {
            return a + b;
        }
    }
}
```

We can now build the solution that will generate the dll file we need. We can now open Unity and see how we can utilize this plugin with Unity:

1. Load Unity, and let's begin by creating a new project. The project will be of type 3D, and the name I will give it is Packtpub. I will start by creating two folders; the first one will be called Plugins, and the other will be called PluginWrappers. This will allow us to keep our project organized:

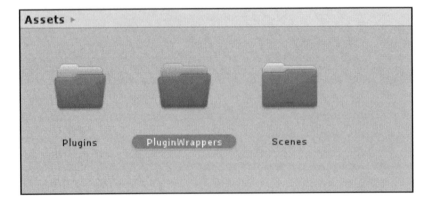

Project setup

2. We will start by taking the C# dll file we created and dragging it into the Plugins folder. I named my dll file CSharpManagedPlugin to make it a bit easier to differentiate between the different plugins we have at the end:

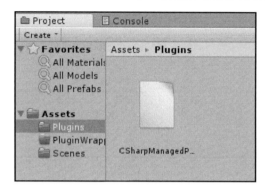

Plugin added

3. If you click on the `CSharpManagedPlugin`, in the inspector, you will see more information:

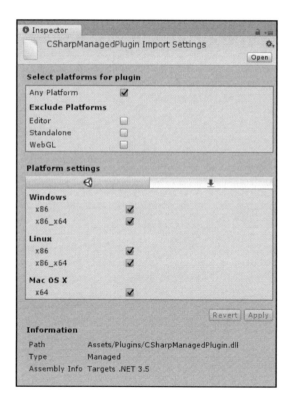

Inspector

4. As long as the target version of .NET is the same or lower than that of Unity, you should receive no errors and should be able to use it in the editor, standalone, in WebGL, Linux, Windows, and Mac OS.

5. What we can do now is move over to our `PluginWrappers` folder and get this bad boy up and running.

6. Create a new script; mine will be called `CSharpWrapper`. We can now open the script in Visual Studio:

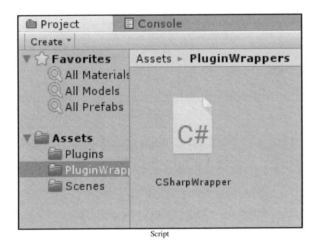

Script

7. Managed plugins are the easiest, and all we need to do is call our plugin directly, just as if it were a non-monobehavior script. Your code should look as follows:

```
using UnityEngine;
public class CSharpWrapper : MonoBehaviour
{
    private void Start()
    {
        var addition = new CSharpManagedPlugin.Addition();
        var add = addition.Addify(5, 2);
        print(add);
    }
}
```

As you can see, we called our plugin as if it were just another namespace in the assembly. We can now attach this Unity class to a GameObject, and we will see the results of step 7 appear in the console window of the Unity Editor.

C++ language plugin

Moving on to C++, we will use Visual Studio once more to create this project:

1. This project type will be in **Visual C++ | Windows Desktop | Dynamic-Link Library (DLL)**:

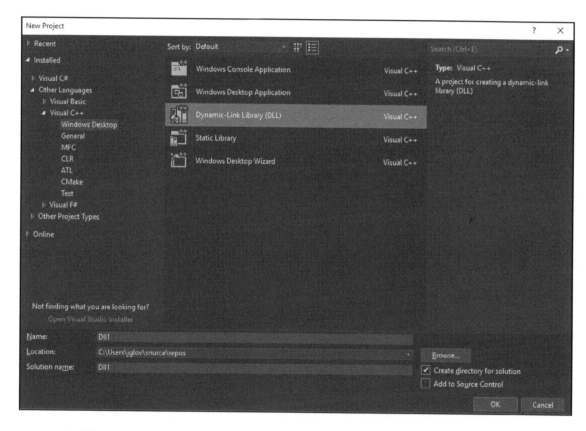

2. The name of this project will be `NativeWindowsPlugin`, and C++ will be slightly different than the managed plugins, due to name mangling, which we will learn how to avoid next.

3. So, to get around this problem of name mangling, we need to create a header and cpp file. Take a look at this code:

   The header will have the extern c and a preprocessor win32 define along with __declspec, dllexport functions to make sure that name mangling does not occur. Again, we will define our public function of addify, which will be our addition function. Your header should look like this.

```
#pragma once
extern "C" {
#if (defined(WIN32) || defined(__WIN32__))
        __declspec(dllexport) int addify(int a, int b);
#else
        int addify(int a, int b);
#endif
}
```

4. Essentially, what is happening when we use the `__declspec`, `dllexport` call is that we are avoiding the usage of a `.def` file.

5. Now that our header has been created, we need to fill out the information in our cpp file.

6. Make sure to include the header for the native windows plugin, and fill out the function details of `addify` here. Your code should look as follows:

```
#include "stdafx.h"
#include "NativeWindowsPlugin.h"
int addify(int a, int b)
{
        return a + b;
}
```

7. Click on **Build Solution**, and we will be ready to jump into Unity.

Load Unity, and let's open our `Packtpub` project:

1. Like we did previously, we will be using our `Plugins` and `PluginWrappers` folders for keeping things organized. Copy the `CPlusPlusPlugin` into the `Plugins` folder:

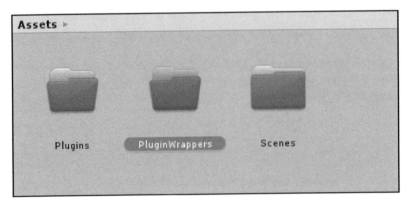

Folder structure

If you take a look at the plugin in the inspector, you will notice that it is only available for Windows. That is because we only had our if directive set for Windows and no other operating system. This is something you should keep in mind when wanting to work with multiple operating systems with C++.

2. Now, we can create a new C# class in the `PluginWrappers` folder called `CPlusPlusWrapper`:

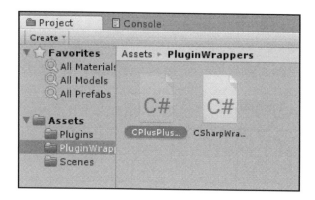

CPlusPlusWrapper

3. The code here will be different than what we used for the native plugin. We will need to import the dll file using a very special attribute called `DllImport`. This attribute requires the string name of the plugin we used and then underneath the attribute, we need to make sure it is a **Public Static Extern Method**.

4. Public static extern method types designate that the method call we want to use will be static, public, and loaded from an external assembly. To use the DLL Import attribute, we need to use the System.Runtime.InteropServices namespace. Your code should look as follows:

```
using System.Runtime.InteropServices;
using UnityEngine;
public class CPlusPlusWrapper : MonoBehaviour {
    [DllImport("CPlusPlusUnManagedPlugin")]
    public static extern int Addify(int a, int b);
    private void Start()
    {
        var add = Addify(2, 4);
        print(add);
    }
}
 }
```

After we do that, the call is essentially the same from there on out. It is a little bit different, and a little more involved, but, overall, it is very easy once you understand how it works. You can now attach this C# script to a GameObject and run it to test the results.

Swift language plugin

Swift Language Plugins have the extension of .swift and have a completely different structure than C#, Java, and C++, which is to be expected, as Swift is only available on macOS devices. The language itself has elements from a variety of sources, and while I will not go into greater details of the finer points of the language, I will say that I like the methodologies they incorporated into the language structure.

Swift and Objective-C require the usage of Xcode, and while the basic setup is very similar, there are some key differences. Swift plugins require you to utilize both Objective-C and Swift to create a plugin that boils down to the implementation in Swift and you call that Swift code in Objective-C. This exceeds the parameters of this section, as the nuances of both languages need to be explored further.

Objective-C language plugin

Objective-C plugins are similar in some ways to Swift plugins and many of the basic steps are the same. Objective-C has been around for quite a long time and was Apple's version of the C language family. While Swift has been designed to be Objective-C's successor, Apple has not depreciated the language and is still a powerful tool to use and know:

1. To start, open Xcode, and get ready to have some fun:

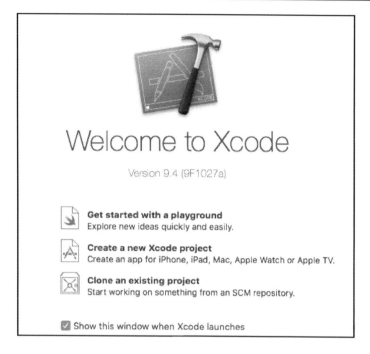

2. Click on **Create a new Xcode project** and we'll have a big list of items to choose from.
3. Go over to **macOS** and select **Library**.

 Although the **Library** is not available with iOS projects, you can also go with Bundle or Cocoa Framework Library types as well for this.

4. Select **Library** and click **Next**:

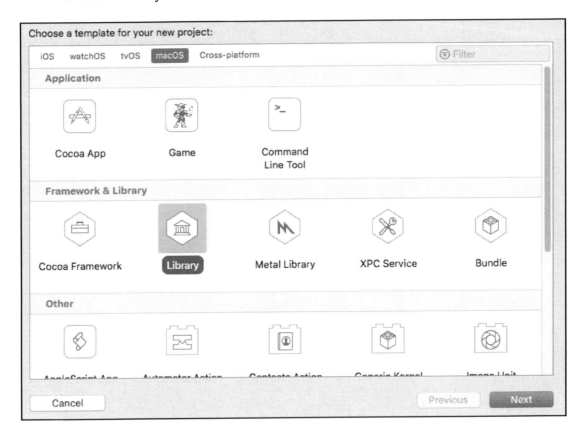

5. Set the product name to `ObjectiveCPlugin`; this keeps us in line with how the projects have been developed thus far:

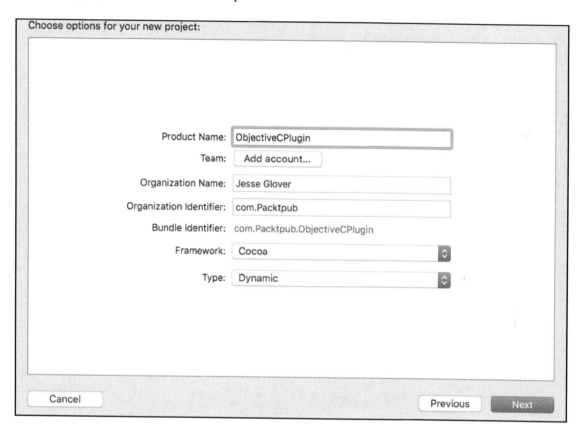

6. Now, before we continue, let's look at the various Frameworks that are available for us in the drop-down menu:

We have **Cocoa**, **STL**, and **None**. Cocoa gives us what we need for Objective C and Swift, **STL** is the **Standard Template Library** for C++, and None is a blank C++ and C project, with no Standard Libraries attached to it. We will stick with Cocoa.

Next, we should take a look at what is available to us with **Type**:

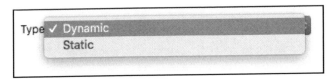

Type gives us the choice between Dynamic and Static, which would be a **Dynamic Library** or a **Static Library**. A static library is a library that is resolved at compile time and copied into a target application that produces an object file and an executable. A dynamic library is the opposite. It is resolved at runtime and only produces the header and source file that can be called in another application or program. We will stick with dynamic here:

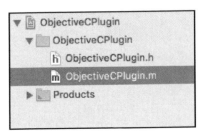

1. Our base Library file has a .h and .m file already created for us, so all we have to do is fill in the code that is needed. Let's go ahead and fill in the header file. Look at this code:

```
#import <Foundation/Foundation.h>
@interface ObjectiveCPlugin : NSObject
int Addition(int a, int b);
@end
```

2. Right away, we can see that it looks very similar to C++, with the slight difference of syntax. Next up, let's take a look at the .m file:

```
#import "ObjectiveCPlugin.h"
@implementation ObjectiveCPlugin
int Addition(int a, int b)
{
  return a + b;
}
@end
```

3. And, again, it's pretty much the same as C++, where we just fill in what the method actually does. We can now build the project and get ready to import it into Unity:

4. Now, we can open Unity after the project has been built and get ready for the fun part. Inside the Plugins folder that we previously created, create a new folder called iOS:

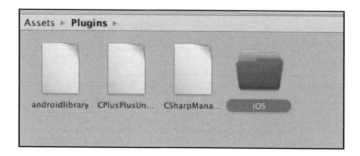

5. Inside the `iOS` folder, copy the `.h` and `.m` files that were created:

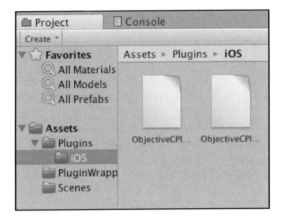

6. Now, go over to the `PluginWrappers` folder and create a new script called `ObjectiveCWrapper`:

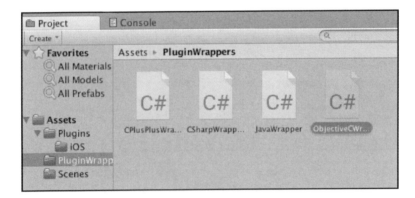

7. We can now open the class in C# and add our code:

```
using System.Collections;
using System.Collections.Generic;
using System.Runtime.InteropServices;
using UnityEngine;
using UnityEngine.UI;
public class ObjectiveCWrapper : MonoBehaviour
{
 private Text text;
#if UNITY_IOS && !UNITYEDITOR
```

```
[DllImport("__Internal")]
public static extern int Addition(int a, int b);
#else
[DllImport("ObjectiveCPlugin")]
public static extern int Addition(int a, int b);
#endif
private void Start()
{
text = GetComponent<Text>();
text.text = Addition(1,5).ToString();
}
}
```

The nice thing about Objective-C is that it does not have the name mangling issues that C++ has, so we don't need to worry about doing the `extern` method before. Instead, due to the way code is compiled for iOS devices, we have to call __internal, instead of the name of the plugin.

To finish, we would have to build this for iOS and open it in Xcode to finish the compile process and either run it on an iPhone or the iPhone Simulator to test the results.

Java language plugin

For the Java language plugin, we have two choices that work just fine. We have the Java Library, which compiles to a JAR file, and the Android Library, which compiles to AAR format. To access Android-specific functions, we need to create the Android Library, and for pure Java language usage, we would create the Java library.

There is a major distinction between the two, and this should be discussed. Consider the following:

- Android Library projects contain native and Java code along with resource files and an Android Manifest. They will include the `.class` files and `.jar` files that need to be precompiled into the Android Studio project, before being imported into Unity.
- Java Library projects are built directly to be JAR files, and they can be imported into Unity.

Both of these plugins need to be run on an Android device; this means you cannot test them in the editor; you must build and run on an emulator or on an actual device. If you want to get the best from plugins, using the Java Language. Android Library projects offer the most bang for your buck.

With that being said, let's open Android Studio and create our basic library:

1. Click on **File**, highlight **New**, and locate **New Module**. The Module options window will open in a new window:

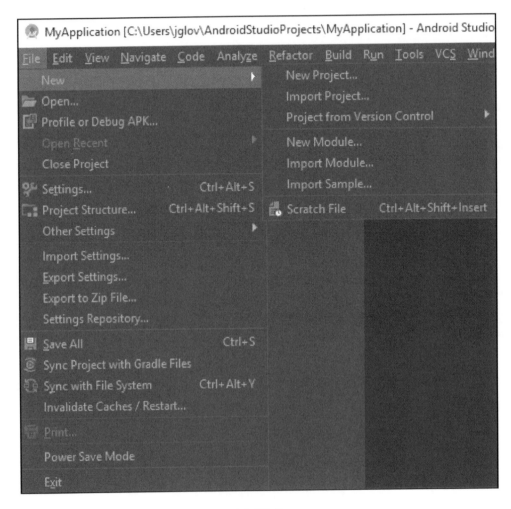

Android Studio

2. Here, we have the option of selecting a **Java Library** or **Android Library**. As discussed previously, it is much more advantageous to use the **Android Library**, so select that one and click **Next**:

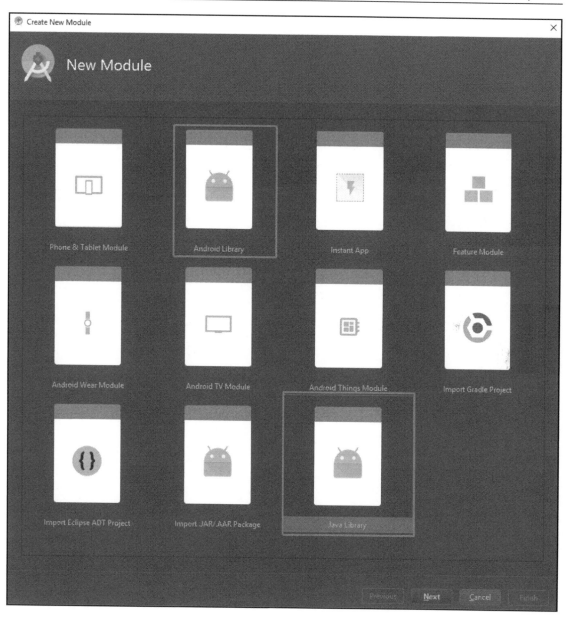

Library choices

3. Now, we can name and configure our module. I will set the library name to be `AndroidLibrary`; the module name will automatically be made to be the name of the library in lowercase.

4. The package name will be changed to `com.packtpub.Androidlibrary`, and the Minimum SDK version will be `API 21: Android 5.0 (Lolipop)`:

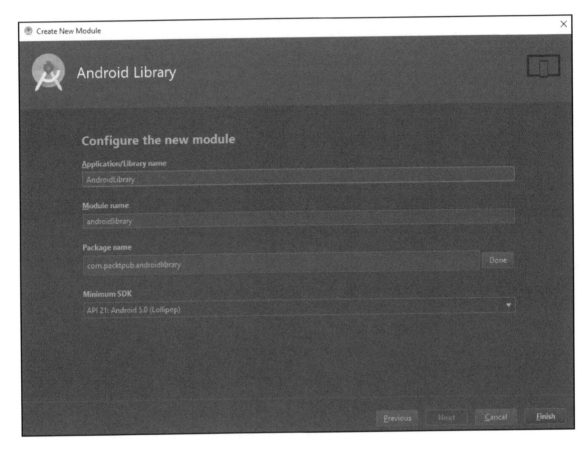

Module setup

5. Once that has been set up, click **Finish**.

6. On the left-hand side of the Android Studio Editor, we can see the layout of the project:

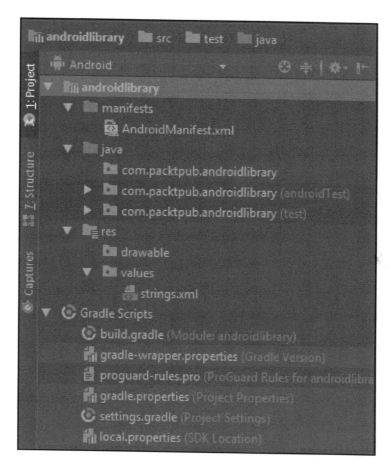

Layout

7. The main area we want to focus on is the `java` folder with the name of `com.packtpub.Androidlibrary`. We need to right-click on this specific one and add a new Java class to it. This will open a brand-new window to set up the class:

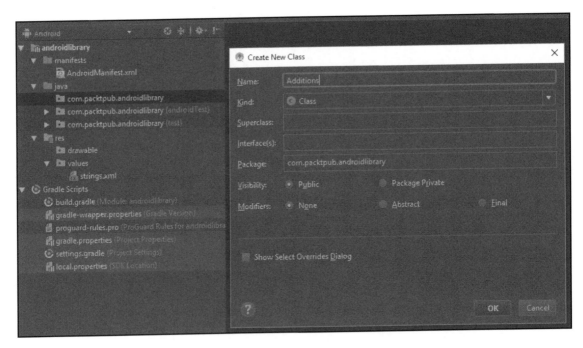

New class

8. I will name the class `Additions` to specify that we are just making a simple math library and then select the **OK** button.

9. The procedure is the same for C#: we will just add a public `int` with the name of `AddMe` with the parameters of `int a` and `int b`, with the return being `a + b`. Your code should look as follows:

```
package com.packtpub.Androidlibrary;
public class Additions {
    public int AddMe(int a, int b)
    {
        return a + b;
    }
}
```

10. Click on the **Build** button at the top of the editor window, and click on **Make Project**. This will build the project for us.

11. Let's take a quick look at the output folder of the project:

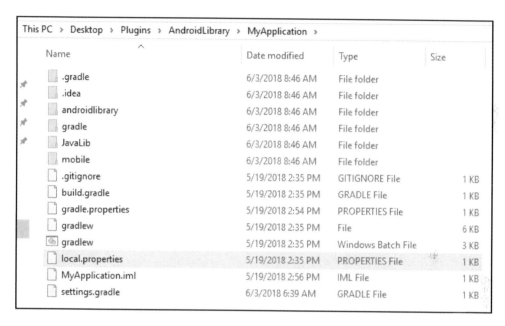

Building the project folder

We can see here that we have quite a few folders and other miscellaneous files. The AAR file we need is located in the `AndroidLibrary` folder. The exact location would be Android library, Build, Outputs, AAR.

The AAR file is technically a zip file, so you can unzip and look at its contents by using "7zip"; however, this is the exact file we need to use in Unity. Now, it is time to open Unity and see how we can get Unity to interact with this file.

Load up Unity, and let's open our `Packtpub` project:

1. Like we did previously, we will be using our `Plugins` and `PluginWrappers` folders for keeping things organized. Copy the AAR file into the `Plugins` folder:

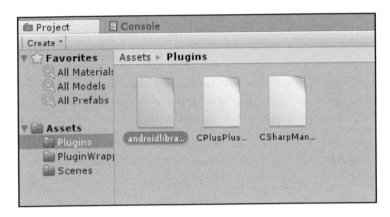

Plugins folder

2. In the `PluginWrappers` folder, create a C# class called `JavaWrapper`, and then open it in Visual Studio.
3. The code is slightly different than the C# and other native implementations. We will need a preprocessor directive to check whether this code is being executed in Android.
4. Then, we will create a new Android Java Object with the string name of the class we created in Java.
5. We will follow that up with a call of that class with the string value of the method we want, followed by the parameters. Your code should look as follows:

```
using System.Collections;
using System.Collections.Generic;
using UnityEngine;
public class JavaWrapper : MonoBehaviour
{
        // Use this for initialization
        void Start () {
#if UNITY_Android && !UNITY_EDITOR
        var javaClass = new AndroidJavaObject("Addition");
        javaClass.Call("Addification", 2, 9);
#endif
}
 }
```

Now, we can't test this code in the Unity Editor, but we can build the project out and test it on an Android device, after attaching it to a game object to run.

Creating a sensor driver in Java

Now, what if we wanted to implement our own sensor from the hardware provided? As it turns out, Google has already thought of that and has a very in-depth tutorial on creating and registering your own driver which can be viewed at https://developer.Android.com/things/sdk/drivers/location. I will go over a few of the items specified, but it is best to read what they wrote.

In short, we will just look at the sample code provided that will make it so that we can convert GPS data as a plugin. The basic structure is exactly the same as the one we used to create our basic plugin in Java. The next step will be to write our code so that it returns the data so that it can be passed from the native plugin to Unity. Take a look at this:

```java
// Convert latitude from DMS to decimal format
private float parseLatitude(String latString, String hemisphere) {
  float lat = Float.parseFloat(latString.substring(2))/60.0f;
  lat += Float.parseFloat(latString.substring(0, 2));
  if (hemisphere.contains("S")) {
  lat *= -1;
  }
  return lat;
}

// Convert longitude from DMS to decimal format
private float parseLongitude(String longString, String hemisphere) {
  float lat = Float.parseFloat(longString.substring(3))/60.0f;
  lat += Float.parseFloat(longString.substring(0, 3));
  if (hemisphere.contains("W")) {
  lat *= -1;
  }
  return lat;
}

// Return a location from an NMEA GPRMC string
public Location parseLocationFromString(String rawData) {
  // Tokenize the string input
  String[] nmea = rawData.split(",");

Location result = new Location(LocationManager.GPS_PROVIDER);
  // Create timestamp from the date + time tokens
  SimpleDateFormat format = new SimpleDateFormat("ddMMyyhhmmss.ss");
  format.setTimeZone(TimeZone.getTimeZone("UTC"));
```

```
    try {
    Date date = format.parse(nmea[9] + nmea[1]);
    result.setTime(date.getTime());
    } catch (ParseException e) {
    return null;
    }

    // Parse the fix information tokens
    result.setLatitude(parseLatitude(nmea[3], nmea[4]));
    result.setLongitude(parseLongitude(nmea[5], nmea[6]));
    result.setSpeed(Float.parseFloat(nmea[7]));

    return result;
    }
```

Now, all you need to do is compile the plugin as specified in the previous section and add it to Unity in exactly the same way.

Summary

In this chapter, we have discussed various sensors that are generally available to us from mobile market devices. We have discussed how to create a basic plugin in the major languages for the different platforms at our disposal, and we now have all of the basic knowledge we need to get started making AR applications and games with Unity.

In the next chapter, we will take what we have learned so far and create a prototype project that will allow us to incorporate sound as the basis for an AR application.

Have a go hero

Before continuing to the next chapter, I would suggest taking the time to read some of the references I have provided in the further reading section that will give you insights on how to access various sensors for Android and Apple devices.

This will be extremely instrumental in you being able to solve the coding challenges presented in the following:

- Create a simple C++ plugin that works with Linux, Windows, and Mac desktop environments
- Create a plugin in Java that will allow the device to actively read the temperature for 10 seconds and display it on your device's screen

- Create a C# plugin that can access your web camera on your laptop, and send that information to the Unity Editor

The following set of challenges are for those that have access to a Mac computer (if you don't, you can modify these to be for Windows or Android):

- Create a Swift plugin that will read a finger press on the screen and log the exact location of the finger press either via text or via display colors on the screen
- Create an Objective-C plugin that takes the information from the camera sensor and logs it in a text file in binary format

Questions

1. Unity is able to utilize plugins from C++:

    A.) True
    B.) False

2. You create your own implementations for handling sensors to inject into Unity via plugins:

    A.) True
    B.) False

3. You can use ARKit to create an Objective-C plugin for Unity:

    A.) True
    B.) False

4. You can build Java plugins to be used with Unity that are targeted at iOS devices:

    A.) True
    B.) False

5. Swift plugins are easier to develop than Objective-C plugins for Unity:

    A.) True
    B.) False

6. The Fingerprint sensor is only available on Android devices:

    A.) True
    B.) False

7. A camera is technically a sensor:

    A.) True
    B.) False

8. A gyroscope is used all the time in iOS and Android devices:

    A.) True
    B.) False

9. A thermometer sensor is used to keep track of and measure the temperature of sensitive components:

    A.) True
    B.) False

10. An accelerometer is not a sensor designed to detect the momentum of the device:

    A.) True
    B.) False

Further reading

The official documentation is always the best place to learn more about the sensors. Check out the following link for more information:

- https://developer.Android.com/guide/topics/sensors/sensors_overview
- https://developer.apple.com/documentation/coremotion
- https://developer.apple.com/documentation/coremotion/cmsensorrecorder

The Sound of Flowery Prose

4

In this chapter, we will design and create our first AR application with macOS and utilize ARKit. This will be an application that utilizes a touch sensor and camera sensors in tandem to initiate sound clips from various literary sources. This will serve as a fantastic introduction to programming and setting up Unity to work with the AR tools available to us. This will also allow us to utilize the built-in functions provided for using the camera sensor and the touch sensor.

In this chapter, we'll cover the following topics:

- Conceptualizing the project
- Setting up the Unity project
- Code implementation details
- Working with XCode

Project overview

The concept of this application is to be able to select anywhere in the video feed of the camera, and it will read a random passage from a poem or book based on the lighting of the area. The build time is approximately 30 minutes.

Getting started

The following are the software prerequisites:

- XCode
- Unity 2018 for Mac
- ARKit
- Visual Studio for Mac
- MonoFramework

The software can be downloaded from the following websites:

- `https://store.unity.com/`
- `https://developer.apple.com/arkit/`
- `https://www.visualstudio.com/`
- `http://www.mono-project.com/download/stable/`

The following are the minimum hardware requirements:

- 2011 or newer Mac computer
- 8 GB of RAM

Conceptualizing the project

Before building any game or application, it should always be a first step to know exactly what you want to build. You don't have to know the exact implementation details, just what you want to build and how you want to go about building it. This should include the following:

- Basic idea/concept
- Programming language to use
- Platform to release on
- Game engine or libraries/frameworks to use
- Design document/design outline
- Written or code implementation prototype for proof of concept

Now, why are these points so important? They are important because it helps solidify the idea, gives a clear path for what you want to accomplish, and most importantly, proves that the project is possible to build. Let's dive into each point and use them to build our first AR application.

Basic idea/concept

The basic idea or concept of an application or game should not be any more than a paragraph explaining what you want to create. It isn't meant to explain the full features or everything you want that to be in the application or game. Rather, it is only meant as a basic starting point that says that this is the overall idea that you want to work on.

This is important because it is the core of the application or game idea, and you can define what the main features of the app or game are and give a clear point of reference for researching.

Our basic concept is to be able to select anywhere in the video feed of the camera and it will read a random passage from a poem or book based on the lighting of the area. Now, this doesn't go too much into depth on what the application will do, but we can use this as the basis for the fourth step to expand upon the basic idea to create a fully functional and detailed explanation of the application.

Choosing the right programming language

This choice is not always obvious when developing an application or a game. While your own knowledge does play a major role in choosing the language to use, so do the requirements of the application or game and your team's knowledge. This step should be done in tandem with the next step before finalizing the decision, as your research may determine that the language that you prefer doesn't have the proper libraries or capabilities for developing the particular game or application you want.

Luckily for us, our example will be using C#.

Choosing your release platform

This one is rather straightforward. Do you want to release on Android, iOS, Windows, or some other platform? This will determine which language to select to use as well as which game engine or libraries/frameworks we need – which leads us to the next section.

Choosing your game engine, libraries, and frameworks

As stated previously, this step should be done in tandem with the previous steps as they are intrinsically tied together. This step requires you to do in-depth and highly detailed research into what you wrote for the basic idea/concept. Not only are you looking to see if what you want to do is possible, but also whether or not the language, game engine, or library/ framework you want to use supports it. This also requires you to know which platform you want to release on.

With the basic idea of this application, we know that it would require utilizing the camera and having touch events to detect whether something is lit well enough or not to determine whether or not it should play the audio file.

Developing the game design and application design document

The design document is more of a design specification document that describes the application in its entirety. That means that all of the data-, architectural-, interface-, and component-level design is described for it. The following example showcases how the documentation would look. You can download a copy of the template from `http://ec.europa.eu/idabc/servlets/Doc7e17.doc?id=18632`:

TABLE OF CONTENTS

Technical design template

For game design, the design document can be a bit more involved than it is for applications. A typical game design document will require the sections described to be filled out in as much detail as possible. You can download a copy of the template from `https://docs.google.com/document/d/1-I08qX76DgSFyN1ByIGtPuqXh7bVKraHcNIA25tpAzE/edit`:

```
Overview
    Theme / Setting / Genre
    Core Gameplay Mechanics Brief
    Targeted platforms
    Monetization model (Brief/Document)
    Project Scope




    Influences (Brief)
        - <Influence #1>
        - <Influence #2>
        - <Influence #3>
        - <Influence #4>
    The elevator Pitch
    Project Description (Brief):
    Project Description (Detailed)
What sets this project apart?
    Core Gameplay Mechanics (Detailed)
        - <Core Gameplay Mechanic #1>
        - <Core Gameplay Mechanic #2>
        - <Core Gameplay Mechanic #3>
        - <Core Gameplay Mechanic #4>
Story and Gameplay
    Story (Brief)
    Story (Detailed)
    Gameplay (Brief)
    Gameplay (Detailed)
Assets Needed
    - 2D
    - 3D
    - Sound
    - Code
    - Animation
Schedule
        - <Object #1>
        - <Object #2>
        - <Object #3>
        - <Object #4>
```

Game design template

Now, you might be thinking that this is a lot of work for applications or games. The key to success is never wrought from laziness or pure luck. In creating documentation that has as much depth as this, you are ensuring that you know exactly what you need to do and why you need to do it, and if you bring on team members, they will be able to read the document and fully understand your goals and intentions with little input from you.

This also means that you can keep yourself firmly in line with the project, forcing you not to add little pet features except as extra milestones after the project has reached the completion mark.

Bonus – UML design

Unified Modeling Language (**UML**) is a great way for visualizing the design of your application or game. NClass is a free UML editor that you can download and use.

You can preplan all of your methods, attributes, properties, classes, and enums – pretty much everything related to programming – with UML. UML really helps for the next phase, which is actually to implement the prototype:

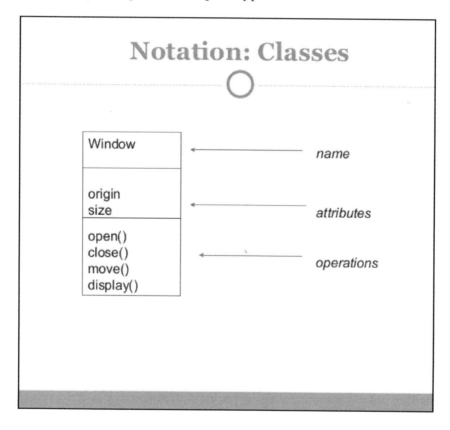

Further planning of implementations can be seen in the following screenshot:

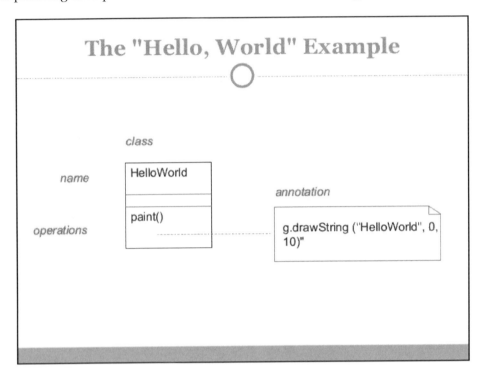

Prototyping

Now, our proof of concept will actually be the full project, although for your own projects in the future, run a small-scale implementation to make sure the features that are 100% necessary are able to be implemented and work appropriately.

The reason for this is that, if for any reason you are unable to implement the main feature of the app or game, you haven't wasted as much time or money on the project as you would have done by implementing on a larger scale.

Setting up the Unity project

The very first thing we are going to do is set Unity up on our Mac computer to be able to create our project. Since we know we will need ARKit, which only works on macOS, we will have different projects for the different chapters, as we don't want any compilation issues:

1. Let's create a new project, and we will call it `Chapter4` or `Sound of Flowery Prose`:

2. Next up, we need to click on the store and search for ARKit to download and add it to our project:

3. I am a bit of a stickler for organization, so we have to make sure to set up all the empty game objects we need to keep things organized. So, we will have four empty game objects called CameraParent, ARKitControl, ARCameraManager, and HitCubeParent. Your project should look like the one in the following screenshot:

4. Drag the camera into the CameraParent empty game object:

5. Create a Cube and drag the Cube into the HitCubeParent object:

Now that we have Unity basically set up as required, we can move on to creating and attaching the scripts we need for the project:

1. Click on the **Camera** component – we have two scripts we need to add to it. The first script is **Unity AR Camera Near-Far**, and the second is **Unity AR Video**.

2. The **Unity AR Video** also needs a clear material, so let's set that to be `YUVMaterial`:

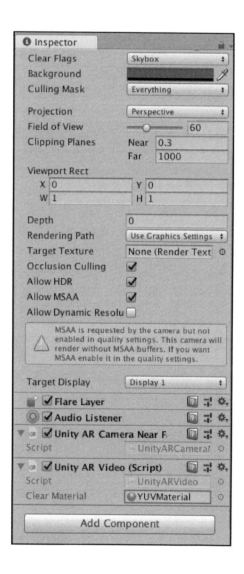

3. `ARCameraManager` needs the appropriate script attached to it – in this case, it is called the **Unity AR Camera Manager**:

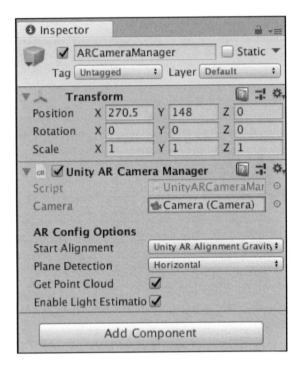

4. `ARKitControl` also needs a script attached to it, and it is called **Unity AR Kit Control**:

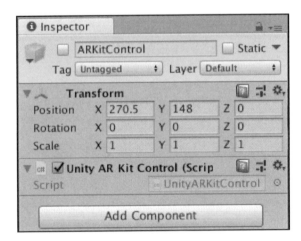

5. The final thing we need to do is set up our `Cube` from inside the `HitCubeParent` object to have a brand new script created for it.

6. Click on the `Cube` object and select **Add Component | Script | New Script**. The name should be `ARHitCube`:

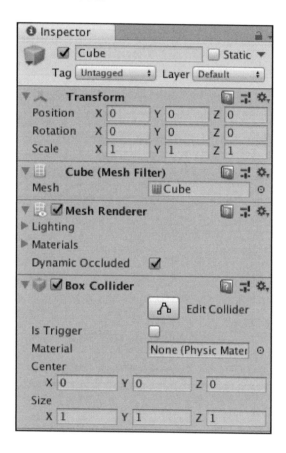

Code implementation details

Obviously, the most important part of any project is actually to implement what we want to accomplish. We want this project to play a literary quote from a list of audio samples automatically. To do this, we need an audio source and audio clips. We also want this project to take advantage of ARKit to run, so we need to write a C# class that utilizes features from the ARKit plugin that is exposed from the Objective-C and C++ libraries.

Let's open up the `ARHitCube` class, fill in the details, and explain what is happening at the same time. I should note that very similar code is already provided in the script file called `UnityARHitTestExample`; I created this script to be able to show only what is needed and to be able to explain the workflow/thoughts necessary for creating the functionality we need:

```
using System;
using System.Collections.Generic;
```

1. As per usual, we will only call the specific namespaces we need for our project. In this case, it is `System` and `System.Collections.Generic`:

```
namespace UnityEngine.XR.iOS
```

2. Our namespace will be used to organize our code to make sure it stays separate from ARKit and Unity's API, which will avoid naming collisions:

```
public class UnityARHitTestExample : MonoBehaviour
{
        public Transform m_HitTransform;
        public AudioClip[] clips;
        public AudioSource source;
```

3. Our class will inherit from `MonoBehavior`, as we want to be able to use it directly from the object (as well as make sure it can be attached to the game object).
4. We create a public transform to allow us to track locations and a public array of audio clips more easily:

```
bool HitTestWithResultType (ARPoint point, ARHitTestResultType
resultTypes)
{
    List hitResults =
UnityARSessionNativeInterface.GetARSessionNativeInterface
().HitTest (point, resultTypes);
```

5. We create a `Boolean` method type that has the parameters of `ARPoint` and `ARHitTestResultType`. Both of these are exposed by ARKit, and you can read the documentation for them or look at the source in Unity to gain a better understanding of it. The simplified explanation is that `ARPoint` is a point coordinate derived from a Vector 3 value, and `ARHitTestResultType` is an enum with the possible results being `ARHitTestResultTypeFeaturePoint`, `ARHitTestResultTypeEstimatedHorizontalPlane`, `ARHitTestResultType EstimatedVerticalPlane`, `ARHitTestResultTypeExistingPlane`, `ARHitTe stResultTypeExistingPlaneUsingExtent`, and `ARHitTestResultTypeExistingPlaneUsingGeometry`.

6. We create a list called `hitResults` which is going to be set to be `UnityARSessionNativeInterface`. `GetARSessionNativeInterface().HitTest` with the parameters being point and result types filled in. What this does is create a list every time a native interface hit test is registered and stores the values:

```
if (hitResults.Count > 0) {
    foreach (var hitResult in hitResults) {
        Debug.Log ("Got hit!");
        m_HitTransform.position = UnityARMatrixOps.GetPosition
(hitResult.worldTransform);
        m_HitTransform.rotation = UnityARMatrixOps.GetRotation
(hitResult.worldTransform);
        return true;
    }
}
return false;
}
```

7. Next up, we do an `if` check to verify that the count is greater than 0. If it isn't greater than 0, return as false, otherwise proceed to the `foreach` loop. Inside of the `foreach` loop, we check all of the hit results and log the results. The `HitTransform` position will always be set to be `UnityARMatrixOps.GetPosition` with the parameter being the `hitresult.worldTransform`.

8. The `HitTransform` rotation will also always be set to be `UnityARMatrixOps.GetRotation` with the parameter being the `hitresult.worldtransform`. We end by returning true. Essentially, all this function does is detect whether a hit is registered or not and passes information to the correct areas that need the information:

```
void Update () {
```

```
/* Let's start the update method as it is probably the second most
important aspect of the code.
*/
 if (Input.touchCount > 0 && m_HitTransform != null)
 {
 var touch = Input.GetTouch(0);
```

9. The first thing we want to do is check whether or not the input.touchcount is 0 and the HitTransform is not equal to null. If either of these checks fails, then we aren't going to be able to retrieve the information we need.

10. We set a touch variable to be input.gettouch with the parameter being 0. 0 is the basic tap gesture:

```
 if (touch.phase == TouchPhase.Began)
 {
 var screenPosition =
 Camera.main.ScreenToViewportPoint(touch.position);
```

11. The if touch phase statement here is a check to see which touch phase is being initialized. The began touch phase is what we want, as it is the starting location of touch events.

12. We created a screen position variable and set it to be the camera screen to viewport point, with the parameter filled out being the touch position:

```
 ARPoint point = new ARPoint
 {
     x = screenPosition.x,
     y = screenPosition.y
 };
```

13. ARPoint point is set to be a new ARPoint, and we want the *x* value to be the screen position's x value and the y value to be the screen position's *y* value:

```
 ARHitTestResultType[] resultTypes = {
 ARHitTestResultType.ARHitTestResultTypeExistingPlaneUsingExtent,
     ARHitTestResultType.ARHitTestResultTypeHorizontalPlane,
     ARHitTestResultType.ARHitTestResultTypeFeaturePoint
 };
```

14. ARHitTestResultType is an array called result types. We want to make sure that the hit test result types are understood, and in this case, we have three types to use: ExistingPlaneUsingExtent, HorizontalPlane, and FeaturePoint:

```
 foreach (ARHitTestResultType resultType in resultTypes)
     if (HitTestWithResultType (point, resultType))
     {
```

```
source.PlayOneShot(clips[Random.Range(0, clips.Length)]);
source.Stop();
return;
}
```

15. We can now do a final `foreach` loop on the `ARHitTestResultType` and create an `if` statement to check the `HitTestWithResultType` with the parameters filled with the point and `resultType`. This essentially just checks to see if the proper touch events have occurred, and if they have, then it activates the play method. Upon another touch event, it will stop the media that was playing. Following that, we return to break from the loop.

16. We can go back to the Unity Editor and look at the cube object's attached script:

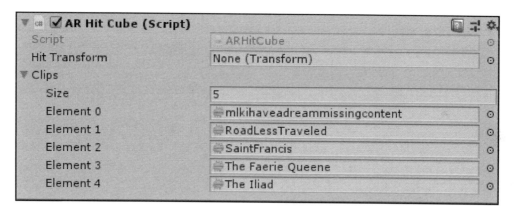

17. We can attach our `Cube` to be the **Hit Transform** as when we tap, this will be the registered object to read the information:

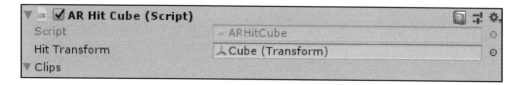

We can now build this project:

1. To do this, click on **File** and **Build Settings**. We will be utilizing iOS as the platform:

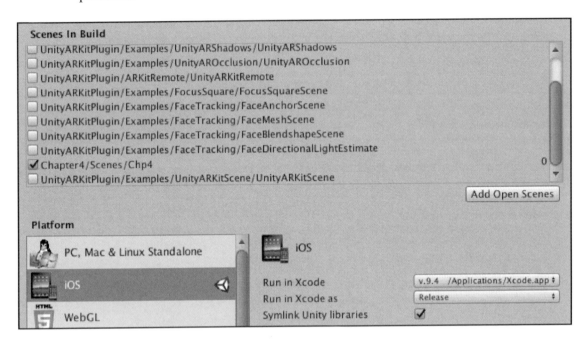

2. In **Player Settings**, we need to change our app's name in the **Bundle Identifier** area and write a small description in the camera usage description.

3. I will name the app com.rpstudios.arkitscene, and the description will be AR BABY:

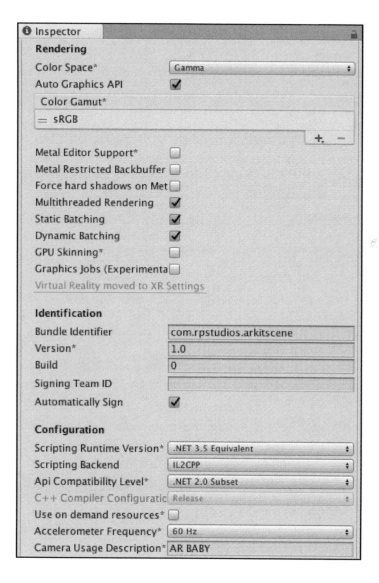

4. Once we select **Build** app, Unity will create an XCode project, which is the main difference between building for Android, Windows, and Linux:

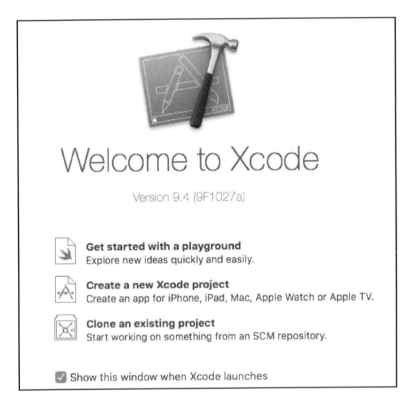

The main bulk of the work is done; now we just need to get familiar with XCode and finalize the build process there.

Working with XCode

We can navigate to the Build folder of our application here and click on it to open our XCode project:

1. On the left-hand side of the screen, you should see **Unity-iPhone** as one of the items you can select. Click on it and you should see **Unity-iPhone** in the center and **Identity and Type** on the right:

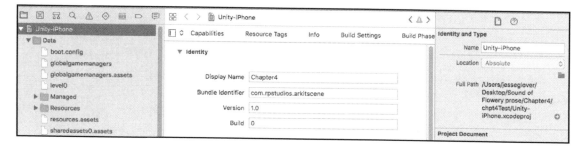

2. Check to make sure the Identity is correct. **Display Name** for me is Chapter4, with the **Bundle Identifier** as com.rpstudios.arkitscene:

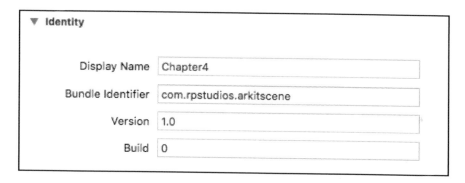

3. Now, on **Signing,** you need to look and make sure that the **Automatically manage signing** checkbox is checked and your **Team** has your email address attached to it. The **Signing Certificate** is extremely important, as you will not be able to compile or send to the simulator properly. If you don't, you have to register for an Apple Developer account at developer.apple.com:

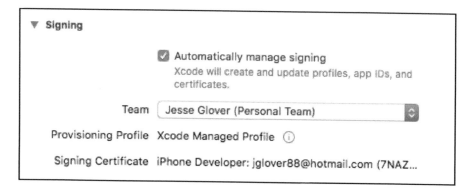

4. Scroll down and look for **Linked Frameworks and Libraries**. **AVFoundation** should be set from **Optional** to **Required**. I've noticed that when it is set to **Optional**, the linker fails to work properly:

▼ **Linked Frameworks and Libraries**

Name	Status
Security.framework	Required ⬍
MediaToolbox.framework	Required ⬍
libiPhone-lib.a	Required ⬍
CoreText.framework	Required ⬍
AudioToolbox.framework	Required ⬍
AVFoundation.framework	Optional ⬍
CFNetwork.framework	Required ⬍
CoreGraphics.framework	Required ⬍
CoreLocation.framework	Required ⬍
CoreMedia.framework	Required ⬍
CoreMotion.framework	Optional ⬍
CoreVideo.framework	Required ⬍
Foundation.framework	Required ⬍
MediaPlayer.framework	Required ⬍
OpenAL.framework	Required ⬍
OpenGLES.framework	Required ⬍
QuartzCore.framework	Required ⬍
SystemConfiguration.framework	Required ⬍
UIKit.framework	Required ⬍
libiconv.2.dylib	Required ⬍
libil2cpp.a	Required ⬍
Metal.framework	Optional ⬍
ARKit.framework	Required ⬍

5. Locate **Architectures**, because we need to change from the default to **Standard**. This is due to there being different architectures and iOS doesn't utilize ARM anymore:

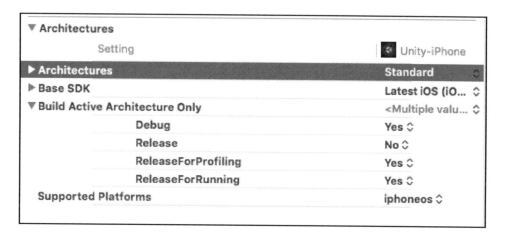

6. Now, you can click on **Build** and attach your iPhone 6 or above to your Mac computer. Build and then run it on the device. It will ask you to trust the app on your phone, so follow the instructions to give trust.
7. Click on the app on your phone and voila! It will load and you can play with the app.

Summary

In this chapter, we learned how to work with ARKit and Unity to build an AR application for Mac devices. While this was a very simple implementation, it should definitely pave the way for you to incorporate different aspects of sound into your own AR games and applications.

Learning the foundations of dealing with AR is possibly the most difficult part, as well as figuring out why building for different devices doesn't work as you intended initially. Debugging and testing is something that should be integral to every aspect of development. I would suggest either having someone test every build, or run automated testing at every chance you get.

In the next chapter, we are going to create an educational-style game prototype aimed at children, which will challenge their cognitive reasoning skills by means of a puzzle.

Questions

1. ARKit comes standard with Unity:

    A.) True
    B.) False

2. You can build for macOS and iPhone on Windows:

    A.) True
    B.) False

3. The bundle identifier can be set to be `app.unity.test`:

    A.) True
    B.) False

4. What is ARPoint and what does it do?

5. The design document is not needed for big projects:

    A.) True
    B.) False

6. UML stands for Uniform Modeling Language:

    A.) True
    B.) False

7. ARKit has built-in VR support:

    A.) True
    B.) False

8. Can you import ARKit into a Unity project on a Windows machine?

    A.) Yes
    B.) No

9. What would happen if you were to use an Objective-C plugin with Windows?

    A.) True
    B.) False

10. Can you use Vuforia and ARKit together in the same project?

    A.) True
    B.) False

Further reading

To understand the different design document templates better, here is a list of places where you can download and look at templates and examples:

- `https://docs.google.com/document/d/`
  `1pgMutdDasJb6eN6yK6M95JM8gQ16IKacxxhPXgeL9WY/edit`
- `https://docs.google.com/document/d/1-`
  `I08qX76DgSFyN1ByIGtPuqXh7bVKraHcNIA25tpAzE/edit`
- `http://robotics.ee.uwa.edu.au/courses/design/examples/example_design.`
  `pdf`
- `https://www.toptal.com/freelance/why-design-documents-matter`
- `http://portal.unimap.edu.my/portal/page/portal30/`
  `BE8D43D77F7A6D38E04400212800D8CE`
- `https://www.cs.drexel.edu/~dpn52/Therawii/design.pdf`

UML is a topic that is discussed in many circles, and there are plenty of resources on it that go into much more depth than I have. The reason for this is that UML could have a book written about it in order to do it proper justice:

- `https://www.utdallas.edu/~chung/Fujitsu/UML_2.0/Rumbaugh--UML_2.0_`
  `Reference_CD.pdf`
- `https://courses.cs.washington.edu/courses/cse403/11sp/lectures/`
  `lecture08-uml1.pdf`

Unity also has some fantastic tutorials where you can learn ARKit with Unity:

- `https://unity3d.com/learn/learn-arkit`

These references should give you deeper insight into topics that I lightly touched on.

Picture Puzzle - The AR Experience 5

In this chapter, we will create another AR-based application. This time, the focus will be a puzzle that could be used in education to teach languages or word recognition. The reason for this is that AR-based applications and games are also very viable sources for inspiration, and target audiences.

This chapter will introduce you to the following:

- How to update an existing installation of Unity to add Vuforia support
- Unity Hub
- How to build an education-based AR app for Windows, Android, and iOS

Let's dive right in and get into the background of this project and why it is relevant to AR.

Project background

As with any other project, it is always best to start with an idea. When I first thought of this project, I wanted to showcase AR applications and games to also reflect education. I have educated children on the English language and know the frustrations of learning a new language intimately.

Game and application development should also teach something to the users; it doesn't always have to be history, mathematics, language, science, or geography; it can also be something innocuous, such as reflex training or hand–eye coordination. We, as developers, have a unique place in the world, being able to incorporate learning something in an engaging way, without it seeming like something the user *has* to do.

This doesn't mean that we have to mull over this and try to incorporate it into our apps and games; it could, and generally is, something that just happens. With this project, though, I have specifically targeted the learning aspect, to show how easily it could be incorporated into AR projects.

Project overview

This project is based on the idea of being able to teach children word association and spelling by creating a really simple puzzle for them to solve in the real world, which they can then check with this app, to find out whether they solved the puzzle.

The build time for this project is 15 minutes at the most.

Getting started

Here are the system requirements for Unity Version 2018.1.5:

- **Released:** 15 June 2018
- **OS:** Windows 7 SP1+, 8, 10
- **GPU:** Graphics card with DX9 (shader model 3.0) or DX11 with feature level 9.3 capabilities.

Check out the following:

https://unity3d.com/
https://www.turbosquid.com/FullPreview/Index.cfm/ID/967597

Installing Vuforia

I know we went over this in `Chapter 1`, *What AR is and How to Get Set up*, but a brief refresher is in order, in case that chapter was skimmed over or Unity has been updated.

To install Vuforia on both macOS and Windows, the steps are quite simple; however, I want to show you a different method of acquiring the Vuforia software and Unity.

Unity has another type of installation you can do called the Unity Hub, which you can get from the Unity website in lieu of the 2018 installer file. What Unity Hub does is allow you to have multiple installations of Unity in a single location, a way to set your preferred Unity Editor, consolidation of your projects into a single launcher, an easy way to update components you want installed, and it also gives you access to templates for project preset types. Follow these steps:

1. Navigate to the Unity website and click on **Get Unity**:

2. You will be presented with an option for **Personal**, **Plus** or **Pro**. Click on **Try Personal** if that fits you and what you need:

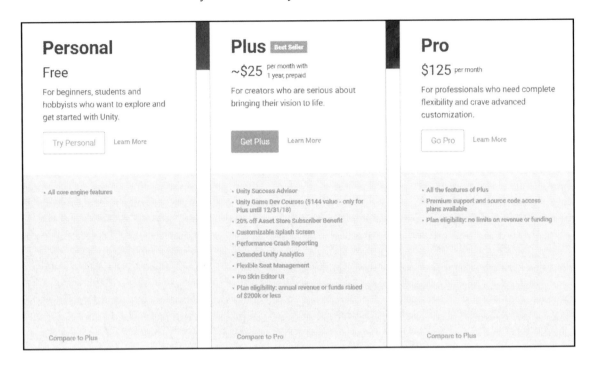

3. That will lead you to the download page, in which you need to put a check mark to accept the terms and give you the option to download the Unity application itself or the Unity Hub that is in Preview. We want the Unity Hub:

Accept terms

☑ **By clicking, I confirm that I am eligible to use Unity Personal per the** Terms of Service, **as I or my company meet the following criteria:**

- Do not make more than $100k in annual gross revenues, regardless of whether Unity Personal is being used for commercial purposes, or for an internal project or prototyping.
- Have not raised funds in excess of $100K.
- Not currently using Unity Plus or Pro.

If you are not eligible to use Unity Personal, please click here to chat with our team about what product is right for you.

| Download Installer for Windows | Download Unity Hub (Preview) |

Looking to download the installer for Mac OS X?
Choose Mac OS X

---

4. Once you have downloaded and installed the Unity Hub, you can open it, and it will give you an option for **Projects**, **Learn**, or **Installs**. Click on **Installs** to look at the available versions:

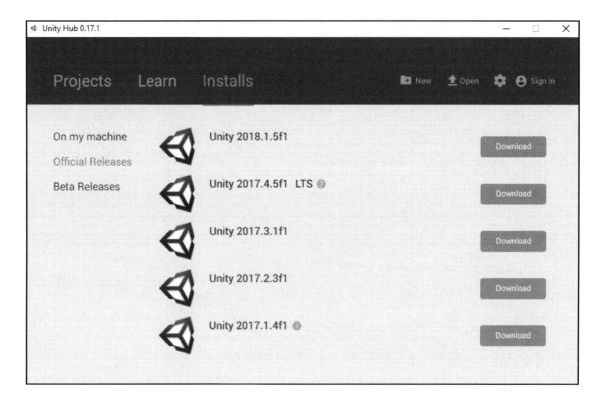

5. We want to install the latest version of Unity, which is 2018.1.5f1:

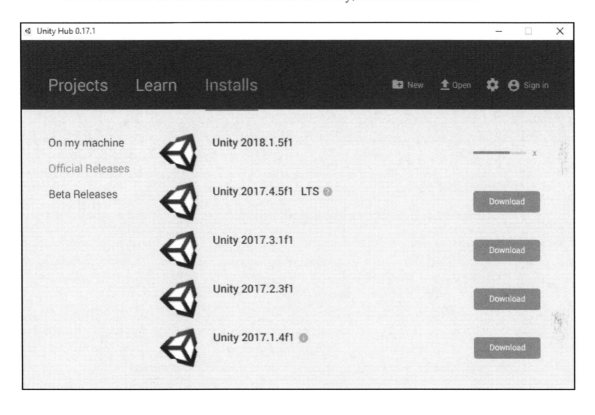

6. Once you click to install the version you want, click on the **Components** you want and press **Done** to install the Unity Editor:

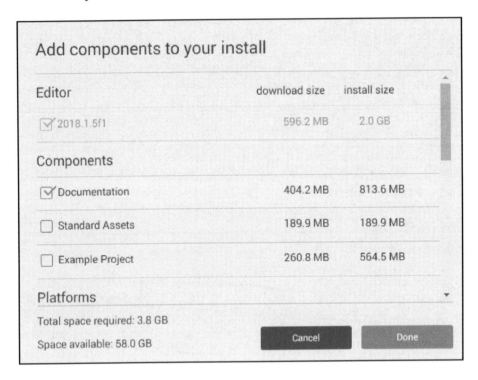

Now, let's say you forgot to select to install Vuforia during this step when you installed Unity—no problem; you can skip the previous points and just follow along from here on out.

7. Open a project in Unity; it could be a dummy project that you don't want, or it could be the basis for this chapter's project.

8. Click on **Build** from the file menu that opens the build menu:

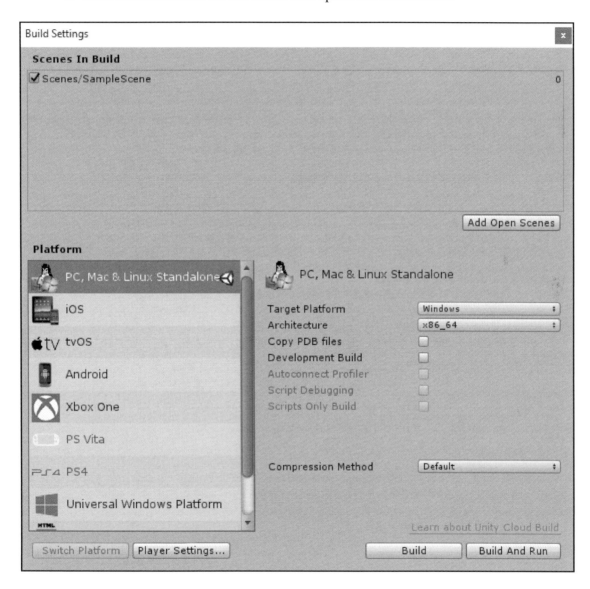

9. We want to select **Player Settings** from this window:

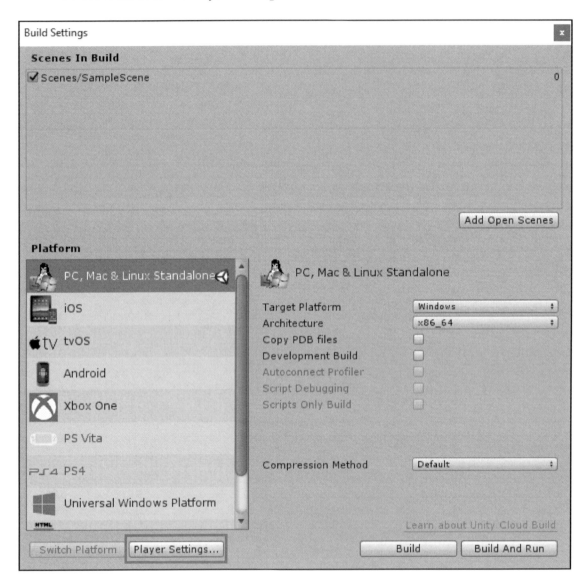

10. The **Player Settings** window should open up where the inspector pane normally is. Locate **XR Support Installers** and click on **Vuforia Augmented Reality**:

11. This will open your browser and ask you to download a file. Click **Save** to download the file:

12. Close the Unity Editor and install this file. This will add Vuforia support to your Unity installation without having to reinstall the entire editor.

Now that this has been completed, we can move on to creating this project in Windows.

Differences between macOS and Windows setups

There is very little difference in the basic setup between macOS and Windows prior to building for their respective platforms. I have set up the projects in the exact same manner so as to make the flow easier to follow. If you own both a macOS and a Windows computer, then when you go to the macOS portion, you can skip to the building section. If you only own Windows, then you can just follow the instructions there. Conversely, if you only own a macOS device, then you will have the full set of instructions there and you can skip the *Windows project setup* section.

Windows project setup

If you remember, in Chapter 1, *What AR is and How to Get Set up*, we created our Vuforia Developer Account. We will need it, as we will be using Vuforia to create this project. Navigate to the Vuforia Developer Portal and log into your account. Now follow these steps:

1. In the Vuforia Developer Portal, click on **Develop**, and make sure the submenu has **License Manager** selected. We need to create a new **Development License Key** with the app name of Chapter5 or Picture Puzzle:

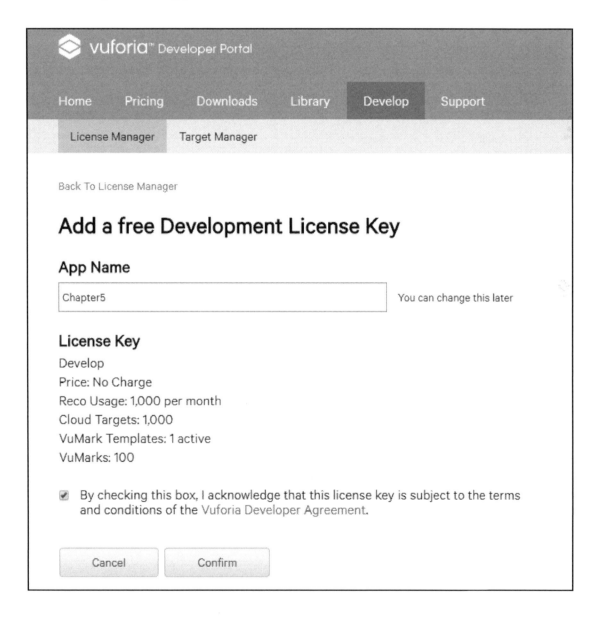

2. After the new key has been created you should see the **License Manager** show the `VuforiaIntro` and the `Chapter5` keys we have created:

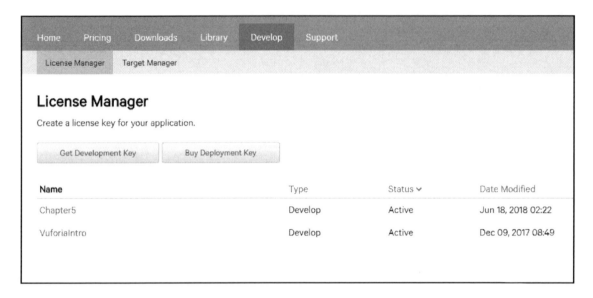

3. Click on `Chapter5` to gain access to your license key. You should copy and paste this into Notepad or Notepad++ for later use:

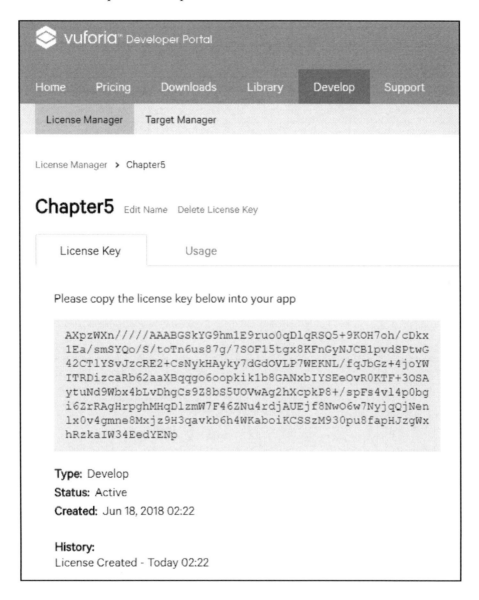

4. Click on **Target Manager**, as we are going to create our own image target for this project:

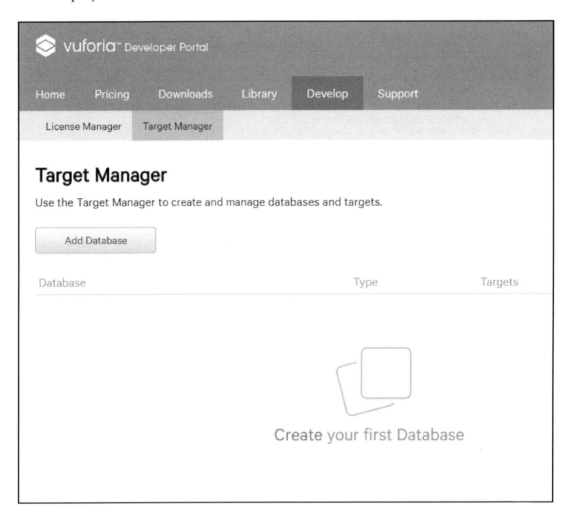

5. Click on **Add Database** to create the brand-new database that we will be utilizing in our project:

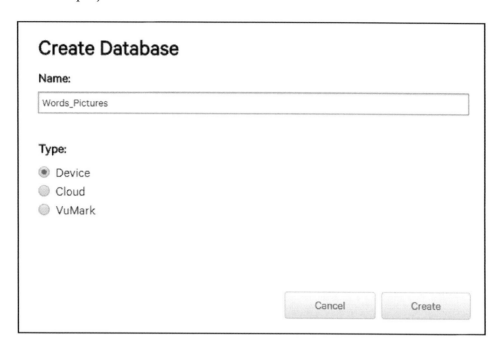

6. You can name the database whatever you want; in my case, I will call it `Words_Pictures`, with the **Type** being **Device**, and click **Create**:

7. It should take us back to the **Target Manager** page and showcase our new `Words_Pictures` database:

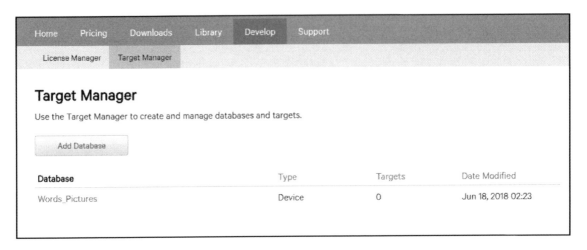

8. Click on `Words_Pictures` to gain access to the database, and then click on **Add Target** when you see it:

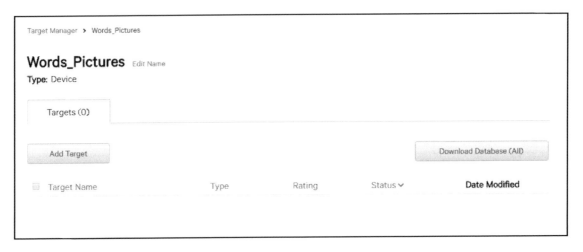

9. We will now be able to add a brand-new target to the database. In this case, we want a single image.

I strongly advise you to create and use a JPG format, as a PNG format requires an 8-bit greyscale image or a 24-bit RGB.

10. The width should be set to the same width as your image. The name should reflect what the image is:

11. Open up Microsoft Paint, and we can begin to create the file that we will use for the target:

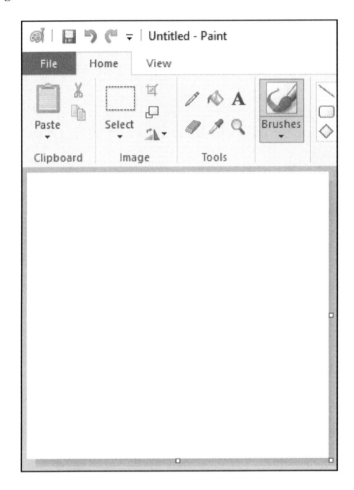

12. The next step is to find the exact size we want to use for this image, and I find the best way to do that is to know what the image is we are going to use. In our case, it will be a **72** in font size, have a font name of **Bastion**, and display the word TREE:

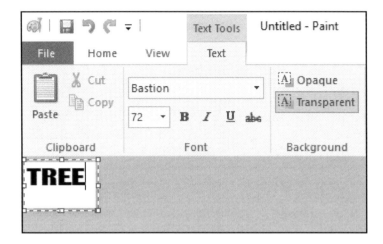

13. Resize the proportions to be close around the edges of the word:

14. Save the file as a JPG and call it `Tree`:

15. If you look at the bottom of the Paint menu, it will tell you the dimensions of the file we just created. In this case it is `253x106`, which is the size we want.

16. Navigate back to the **Add Target** web page and choose the `Tree` file we just created:

17. Set the width to be `253` and the name to `Tree`, and then click **Add**:

18. It will take you back to the database, and you should see the `TreeWord` with `Tree` as the name. The type should be **Single Image**, and there should be a three-star rating:

	Target Name	Type	Rating	Status ⌄	Date Modified
☐ TREE	Tree	Single Image	★★★☆☆	Active	Jun 19, 2018 02:57

19. The rating system is designed to tell you whether it is of the proper size to be read correctly by your AR device. We currently have a three-star rating, which means that it should be good, but it could be much better. What can we do to fix this? We can enlarge the image.

20. Let's delete the image from the database. To do this, click on the little checkbox next to `Tree`, and above it will appear a very small **Delete** button:

21. Let's go back to Paint and resize the image. 680 by 480 should be perfect, although 500x300 will work as well:

22. Upload the new target, and the results should have a five-star rating:

	Tree	Untitled	Single Image	★★★★★	Active	Jun 18, 2018 02:38

23. Click on **Download Database (All)**:

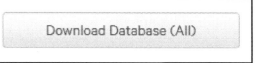

24. This will open a new window that will ask us which development platform we want to utilize this with. We want Unity Editor. Click **Download**:

It will download a Unity file that we will need to import into our Unity Project—which, now, we can begin to work with in Unity, without having to leave the editor to do any other work. Open Unity, and let's begin building our project.

Building the Windows project

Create a new Unity Project, if you haven't already, and call it Chapter5 to begin with. Then load the project.Now follow these steps:

1. The Words_Pictures file that we downloaded now needs to be located and imported into the project:

2. Before we dive in and create the project, let's have a look at the folders that were created upon import.

3. Our main `Assets` folder will now have an `Editor` folder, a `StreamingAssets` folder and a `Scenes` folder:

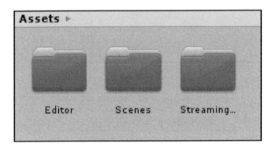

4. Inside the `Editor` folder, it will have another folder called `Vuforia`:

5. Inside the `Vuforia` folder will be another folder called `ImageTargetTextures`:

6. Inside the `ImageTargetTextures` folder, there will be a folder called `Word_Pictures`:

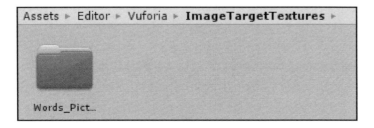

7. The `Word_Pictures` folder will contain our tree image sprite:

8. Go back to the main `Assets` folder, and let's take a look, starting with `StreamingAssets`:

9. Inside the `StreamingAssets` folder will be a `Vuforia` folder:

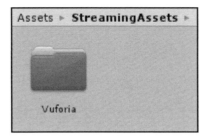

10. Inside the `Vuforia` folder will be two files: `Words_Pictures.xml` and `Words_Pictures.dat` file:

11. Let's take a look at the XML file in depth to see what exactly is in it. Take a look at this code:

```
<?xml version="1.0" encoding="UTF-8"?>
<QCARConfig xmlns:xsi="http://www.w3.org/2001/XMLSchema-instance"
xsi:noNamespaceSchemaLocation="qcar_config.xsd">
  <Tracking>
    <ImageTarget name="Tree" size="680.000000 480. 000000" />
  </Tracking>
</QCARConfig>
```

The XML file has the default schema for it set up, with the main tag being `QCarconfig`.

The next tag, which houses our image, is `ImageTarget`. It has the name, which we set to `Tree` and the size written in floating-point values.

The XML file is very short and to the point. This file is specifically for housing the data that Vuforia needs to know, the size of the images we are using, and to be able to reference the proper file if we were to have multiple images. Continue to follow the steps:

12. Go to the TurboSquid website and download the free `Tree` model that we will be using:

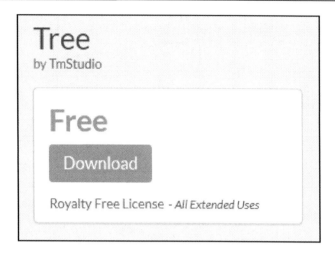

13. You will need the `Tree_FBX` and the `Tree_textures` files for this next portion:

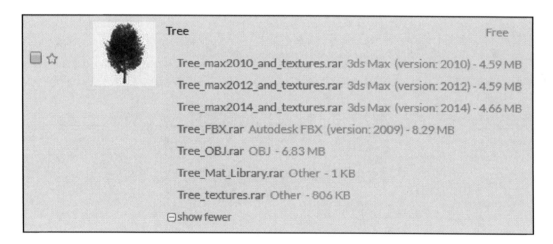

14. Navigate back to the main `Assets` folder and create a new folder called `Models`:

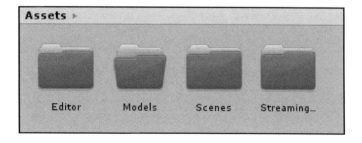

15. Extract both the tree model and the textures. Copy and paste the model and textures into the `Models` folder inside Unity:

16. Delete the standard camera from the hierarchy pane.
17. Right-click in the hierarchy pane and navigate to **Vuforia**; click to add an **AR Camera**:

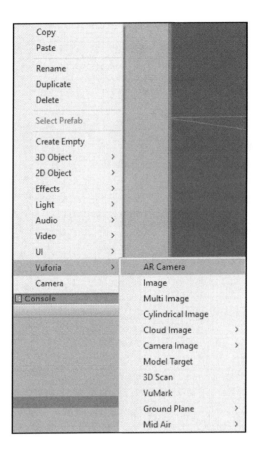

18. Click on the `AR Camera` in the hierarchy pane. Look over to the **Inspector** pane and click on **Open Vuforia Configuration**:

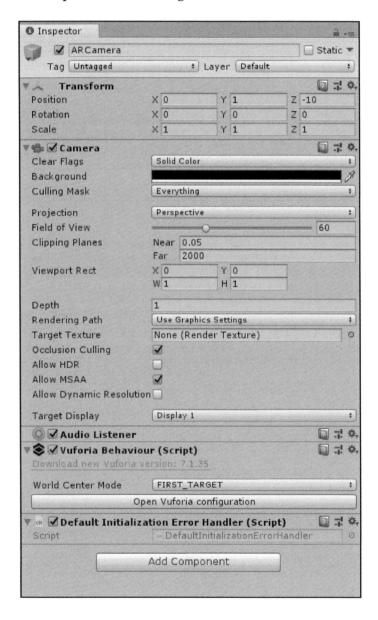

19. Unity should ask for you to import and download more items for Vuforia and accept the Vuforia license:

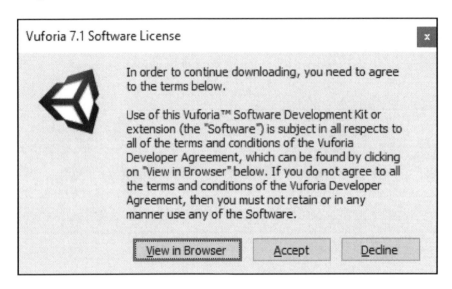

20. Copy and paste your app license key into the **App License Key** section:

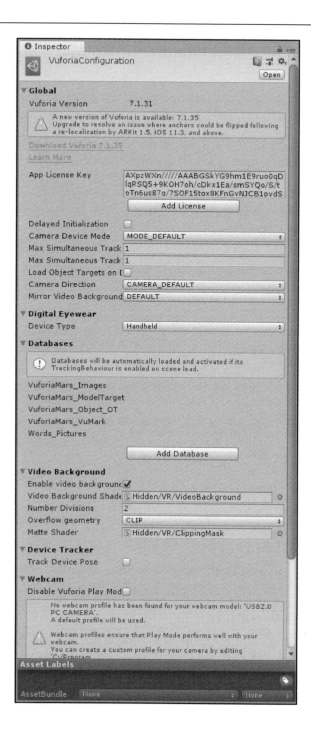

21. Right-click on the hierarchy pane and create an empty game object called
    `ImageTarget`.

22. Right-click on the `ImageTarget` object and highlight **Vuforia** and click on
    Image:

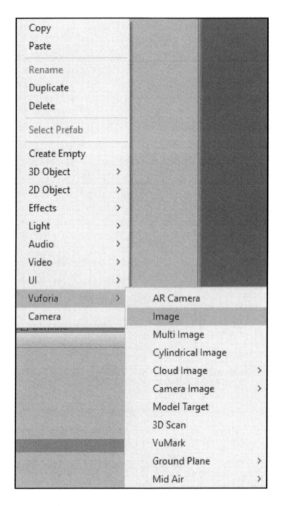

23. Click on the **Image** object and look at the **Inspector** pane. **Image Target Behavior**
    should have the type be **Predefined**; the **Database** should be **Words_Pictures**,
    and the **Image Target** should be **Tree**:

Now we need to add our model. I am assuming you know how to set up materials for the model, so I will not go over it here.

24. Drag and drop the model on to the scene. Set the *x*, *y*, and *z* positions to be 0,0,0, with the scale being 0.09 for the *x*, *y*, and *z* coordinates. The last thing to do is make it a child of the image inside the **ImageTarget** object:

25. Print out the Tree text and cut the paper into four strips.
26. Build the project for a **PC, Mac & Linux Standalone** or **Android** by clicking on **File | Build Settings**, and click on **Build**:

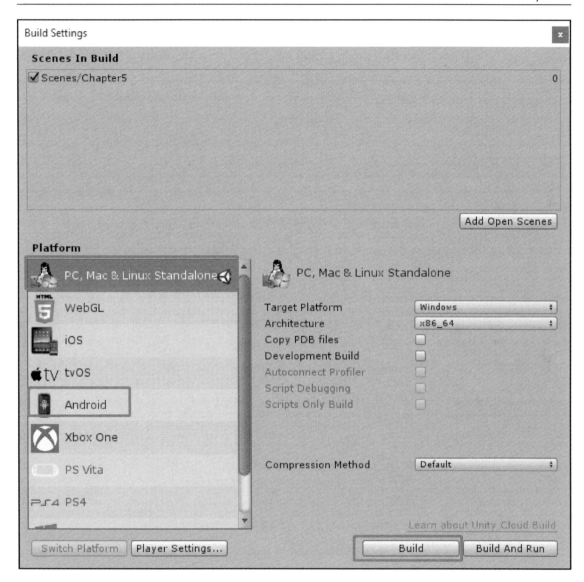

Now with your Android device or PC camera being utilized, put the strips together in the proper order, and the `Tree` model will appear over the top of the paper.

macOS project setup

The steps for setting up the project in Mac are nearly identical, with the difference mainly being the software we will use to create the text file, but, nonetheless, this should be gone over, as I expect Mac users will not want to read the Windows section of this chapter. We will need it, as we will be using Vuforia to create this project. Navigate to the Vuforia Developer Portal and log into your account. Now follow these steps:

1. In the Vuforia Developer Portal, click on **Develop**, and make sure the submenu has **License Manager** selected. We need to create a new **Development License Key** with the app name of Chapter5:

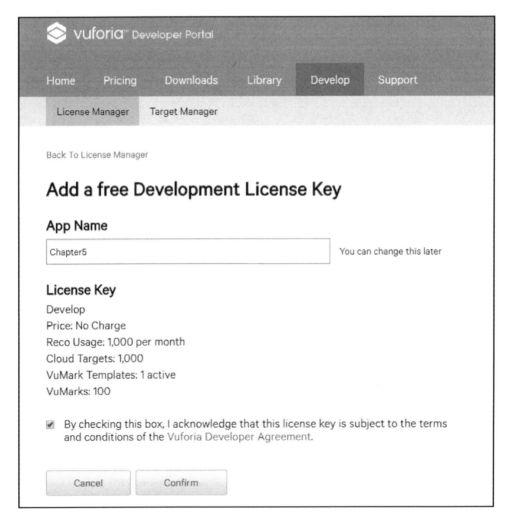

2. After the new key has been created, you should see the **License Manager** show the VuforiaIntro and the Chapter5 keys we have created:

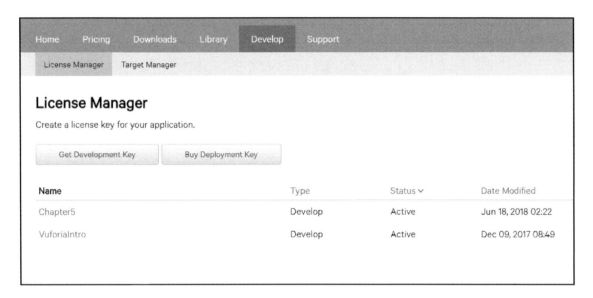

3. Click on `Chapter5` to gain access to your license key. You should copy and paste this into Notepad or Notepad++ for later use:

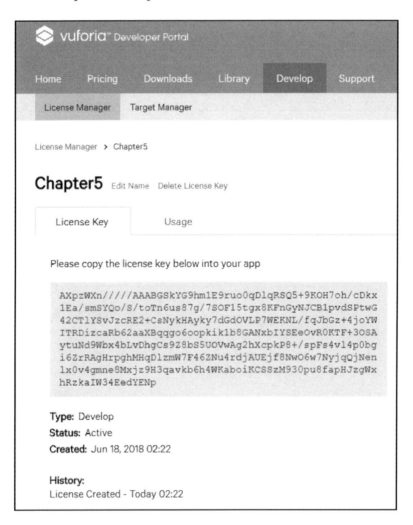

4. Click on **Target Manager**, as we are going to create our own image target for this project:

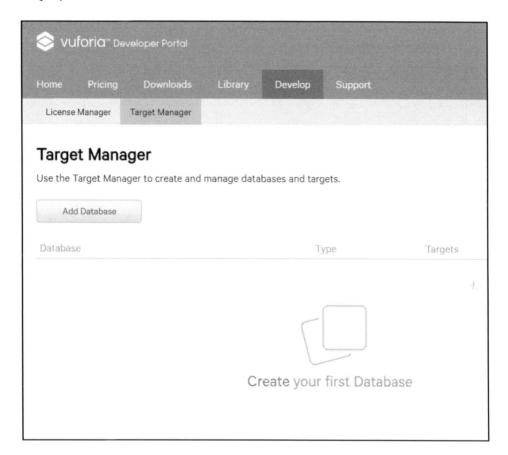

5. Click on **Add Database** to create the brand-new database that we will be utilizing in our project:

6. You can name the database whatever you want; in my case, I will call it `Words_Pictures`, with the **Type** being **Device**, and click **Create**:

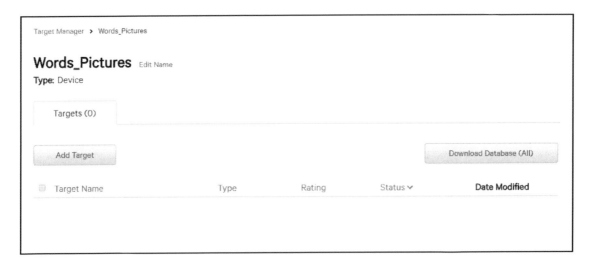

7. It should take us back to the **Target Manager** page and showcase our new `Words_Pictures` database:

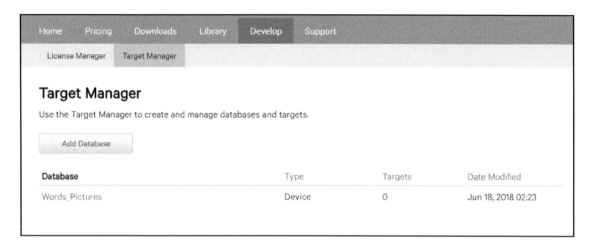

8. Click on `Words_Pictures` to gain access to the database, and then click on **Add Target** when you see it:

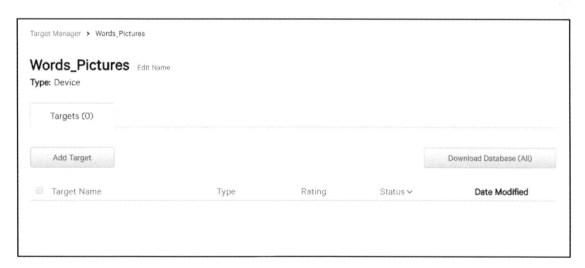

9. We will now be able to add a brand-new target to the database. In this case, we want a single image.

I strongly advise you to create and use a JPG format, as a PNG format requires an 8-bit greyscale image or a 24-bit RGB.

10. The width should be set to the same width as your image. The name should reflect what the image is:

11. Open Microsoft Paint, and we can begin to create the file that we will use for the target:

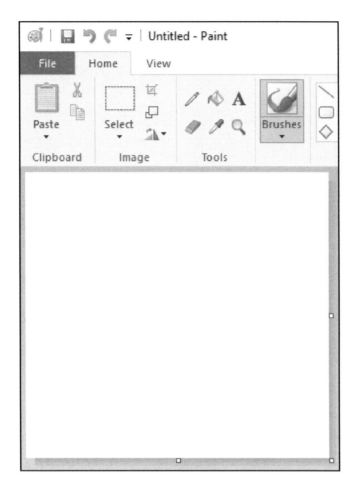

12. The next step is to find the exact size we want to use for this image, and I find the best way to do that is to know what the image is we are going to use. In our case, it will be **72** in font size, have the font name of **Bastion**, and display the word `Tree`:

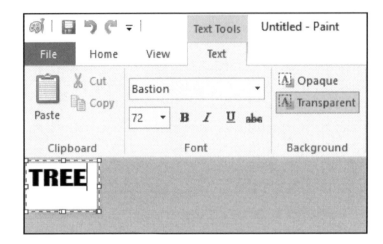

13. Resize the proportions to be close around the edges of the word:

14. Save the file as a JPG and call it `Tree`:

15. If you look at the bottom of the Paint menu, it will tell you the dimensions of the file we just created. In this case it is `253x106`.

16. Navigate back to the **Add Target** web page and choose the `Tree` file we just created:

17. Set the width to be 253 and the name to be **Tree**, and then click on **Add**:

18. It will take you back to the database, and you should see the word `Tree`, with the **Name** as `Tree`, **Type** as **Single Image**, and there should be a three-star rating:

	Target Name	Type	Rating	Status ∨	Date Modified
☐ **TREE**	Tree	Single Image	★★★☆☆	Active	Jun 19, 2018 02:57

The rating system is designed to tell you whether it is of the proper size to be read correctly by your AR device. We currently have a three-star rating, which means that it should be good, but it could be much better. What can we do to fix this? We can enlarge the image. Let's continue following the steps:

19. Let's delete the image from the database. To do this, click on the little checkbox next to `Tree`, and above it will appear a very small **Delete** button:

20. Let's go back to Paint and resize the image. `680` by `480` should be perfect:

21. Upload the new target, and the results should have a five-star rating:

| ☐ Tree | Untitled | Single Image | ★ ★ ★ ★ ★ | Active | Jun 18, 2018 02:38 |

22. Click on **Download Database (All)**:

23. This will open a new window that will ask which development platform we want to utilize this with. We want Unity Editor. Click **Download**:

It will download a Unity file that we will need to import into our Unity Project—which, now, we can begin to work in Unity, without having to leave the editor to do any other work. Open Unity, and let's begin building our project.

Building the macOS Project

Create a new Unity Project, if you haven't already, and call it Chapter5 to begin with. Then, load the project. Now follow these steps:

1. The Words_Pictures file that we downloaded now needs to be located and imported into the project.
2. Before we dive in and create the project, let's have a look at the folders that were created upon import. Our main Assets folder will now have an Editor folder, a StreamingAssets Folder, and a Scenes folder:

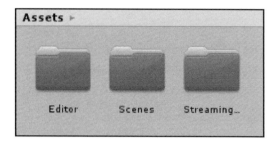

3. Inside the Editor folder, it will have another folder called Vuforia:

4. Inside the Vuforia folder will be another folder called ImageTargetTextures:

5. Inside the ImageTargetTextures folder, there will be a folder called Word_Pictures:

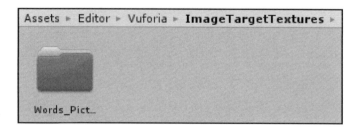

6. Inside the `Word_Pictures` folder, we will have our tree image sprite:

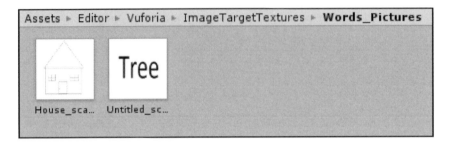

7. Go back to the main `Assets` folder and let's take a look, starting with `StreamingAssets`:

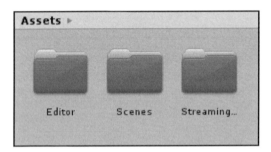

8. Inside the `StreamingAssets` folder will be a `Vuforia` folder:

9. Inside the `Vuforia` folder will be two files: `Words_Pictures.xml` and `Words_Pictures.dat`:

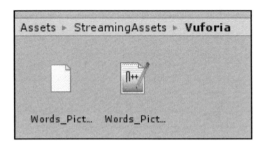

10. Let's take a look at the XML file in depth to see what exactly is in it:

```
<?xml version="1.0" encoding="UTF-8"?>
<QCARConfig xmlns:xsi="http://www.w3.org/2001/XMLSchema-instance"
xsi:noNamespaceSchemaLocation="qcar_config.xsd">
  <Tracking>
    <ImageTarget name="Tree" size="680.000000 480. 000000" />
  </Tracking>
</QCARConfig>
```

The XML file has the default schema for it set up, with the main tag being `QCarconfig`.

The next tag, which houses our image, is `ImageTarget`. It has the name, which we set to `Tree`, and the size written in floating-point values.

The XML file is very short and to the point. This file is specifically for housing the data that Vuforia needs to know, the size of the images we are using, and to be able to reference the proper file if we were to have multiple images. Let's continue with the steps:

11. Go to the TurboSquid website and download the free `Tree` model that we will be using:

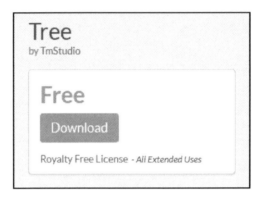

12. You will need the `Tree_FBX` and the `Tree_textures` files for this next section:

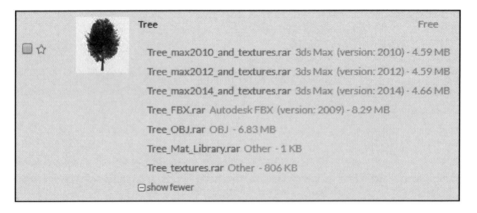

13. Navigate back to the main `Assets` folder and create a new folder called `Models`:

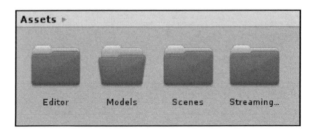

14. Extract both the tree model and the textures. Copy and paste the model and textures into the `Models` folder inside of Unity:

15. Delete the standard camera from the hierarchy pane.
16. Right-click in the hierarchy pane and navigate to **Vuforia**; click to add an **AR Camera**:

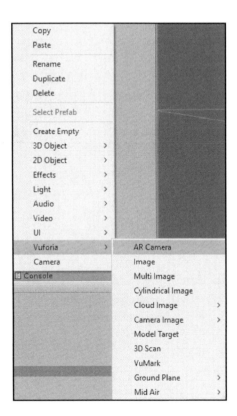

17. Click on the AR Camera in the hierarchy pane. Look over to the **Inspector** pane and click on **Open Vuforia Configuration**:

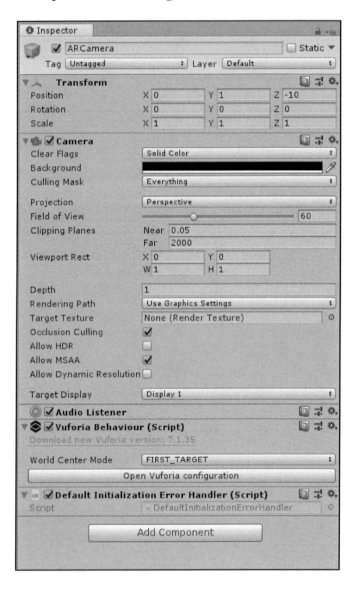

18. Unity should ask for you to import and download more items for Vuforia and accept the Vuforia license:

19. Copy and paste your app license key into the **App License Key** section:

20. Right-click on the hierarchy pane and create an empty game object called `ImageTarget`.

21. Right-click on the `ImageTarget` object and highlight **Vuforia**, and click on **Image**:

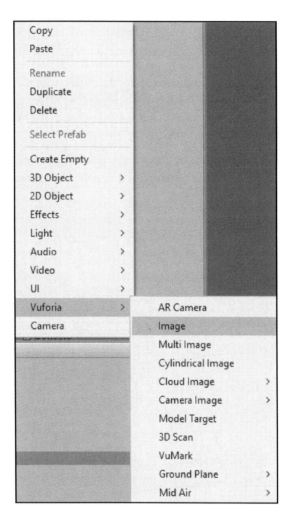

22. Click on the `Image` object and look at the **Inspector** pane. **Image Target Behavior** should have the **Type** as **Predefined**. Database should be **Words_Pictures** and **Image Target** should be **Tree**:

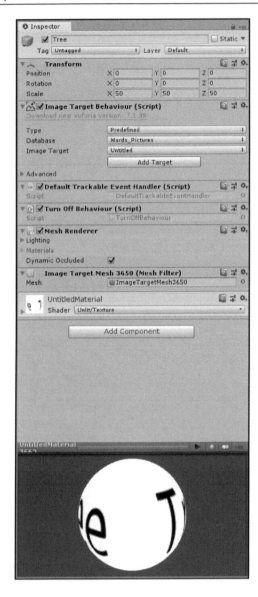

Now we need to add our model. I am assuming you know how to set up materials for the model, so I will not go over it here. Let's continue with the steps:

23. Drag and drop the model on to the scene. Set the *x*, *y*, and *z* positions to be 0,0,0, with the scale being 0.09 for the *x*, *y*, and *z* coordinates. The last thing to do is make it a child of the image inside the **ImageTarget** object:

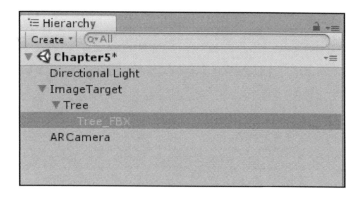

24. Print out the `Tree` text and cut the paper into four strips.

25. Build the project for **iOS** by clicking on **File | Build Settings**. Make sure to select the **Development Build** check mark:

Working with Xcode

We can navigate to the `Build` folder of our application here, and click on it to open our XCode project. Follow these steps:

1. On the left-hand side of the screen, you should see `Unity-iPhone` as one of the items you can select. Click on it and you should see **Unity-iPhone** in the center and **Identity and Type** on the right:

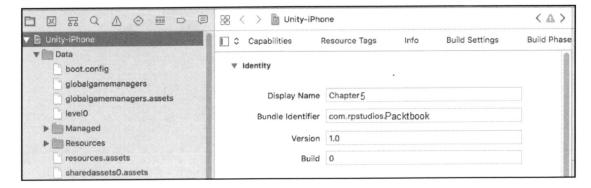

2. Check to make sure the **Identity** is correct. The **Display Name** for me is Chapter5, with the **Bundle Identifier** as com.rpstudios.Packtbook:

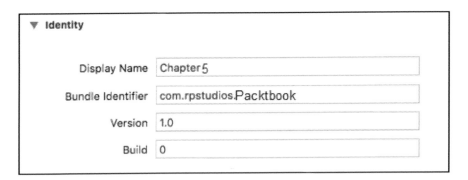

3. Now, on **Signing,** you need to look and make sure that the **Automatically manage signing** checkbox is checked and that **Team** has your email address attached to it:

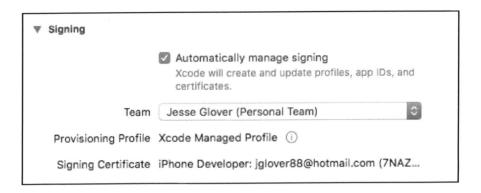

4. Scroll down and look for **Linked Frameworks and Libraries**. AVFoundation should be set from **Optional** to **Required**. I've noticed that when it is set to **Optional**, the linker fails to work properly:

▼ **Linked Frameworks and Libraries**

Name	Status
Security.framework	Required ↕
MediaToolbox.framework	Required ↕
libiPhone-lib.a	Required ↕
CoreText.framework	Required ↕
AudioToolbox.framework	Required ↕
AVFoundation.framework	Optional ↕
CFNetwork.framework	Required ↕
CoreGraphics.framework	Required ↕
CoreLocation.framework	Required ↕
CoreMedia.framework	Required ↕
CoreMotion.framework	Optional ↕
CoreVideo.framework	Required ↕
Foundation.framework	Required ↕
MediaPlayer.framework	Required ↕
OpenAL.framework	Required ↕
OpenGLES.framework	Required ↕
QuartzCore.framework	Required ↕
SystemConfiguration.framework	Required ↕
UIKit.framework	Required ↕
libiconv.2.dylib	Required ↕
libil2cpp.a	Required ↕
Metal.framework	Optional ↕
ARKit.framework	Required ↕

5. Locate **Architectures**, because we need to change from the default to **Standard**. This is due to there being different architectures and iOS doesn't utilize ARM anymore:

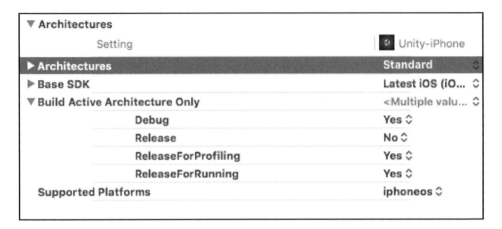

6. Now you can click on **Build** and attach your iPhone 6 or above to your macOS computer. **Build** and then run it on the device. It will ask you to trust the app on your phone, so follow the instructions to give trust.
7. Click on the app on your phone and—voila!—it will load, and you can play with the app.

Now with your iOS device being utilized, put the strips together in the proper order, and the Tree model will appear over the top of the paper.

Summary

In this chapter, we learned how to create an educational game for children so they can learn what objects are in relation to the words for them. We learned how to develop using Vuforia, for both macOS and Windows for Android and iOS devices. We also learned that the basic building blocks for building on Windows and macOS devices are fairly similar code-wise, the only major difference being the extra steps required to compile to iOS or macOS, using XCode.

In the next chapter, we will build a prototype of a fitness application designed to allow the user to randomly select the location of where they want to walk, for fun.

Questions

1. To install Vuforia for Unity, you have to go to the Vuforia website to download the SDK:

   A.) True
   B.) False

2. You need to install the legacy plugin for the 2017 version of Unity:

   A.) True
   B.) False

3. The Unity Hub makes it easy to have multiple versions of Unity installed:

   A.) True
   B.) False

4. Microsoft Paint can make the PNG and JPG files needed for the Vuforia image targets:

   A.) True
   B.) False

5. Vuforia Image Targets can accept the TIFF file format:

   A.) True
   B.) False

6. Vuforia's file size limit for PNG and JPG files is 5 MB:

   A.) True
   B.) False

7. Vuforia is not available on macOS:

   A.) True
   B.) False

8. Unity Hub is available on macOS and Windows:

   A.) True
   B.) False

9. The star rating system in the Vuforia Database is for how good the quality of an image is:

A.) True
B.) False

10. You don't need a Vuforia license key to use it with Unity:

A.) True
B.) False

Fitness for Fun - Tourism and Random Walking

6

In this chapter, we will utilize Mapbox to create an AR fitness application prototype. The reason for this is that the main focus will be utilizing GPS, geolocation, and the Android/Apple device hardware to communicate with satellites and receive that data. Mapbox is an SDK designed to utilize the geolocation features of both Android and Apple devices within Unity. The software we will use in conjunction with Unity to make this happen much more seamlessly is Mapbox. Mapbox takes care of a lot of the most difficult portions of the work, so we only have to focus on our games and applications that utilize the software. We will learn how to use Mapbox with Unity to create a fitness application that promotes walking around the area in which you live. Basically, the user will tap on a random location and it will set the destination as that location. The user will then have to walk to that location, which will trigger the destruction of that marker.

In this chapter, we will cover the following topics:

- Learning about Mapbox
- Integrating Mapbox into Unity
- Implementing Mapbox data into an AR application

Background information on Mapbox

Mapbox allows you to create Location Based, City Simulators, TabletopAR and WorldScaleAR applications and games. For any project you have that might require geolocation, Mapbox is the software to utilize. Mapbox was built from the ground up to be compatible with Unity, Android, and iOS.

Mapbox is free for web and mobile SDKs for up to 50,000 map views, geocode requests, direction requests, and matrix elements per month. After reaching the 50,000 limit, there is a charge of 0.5 cents per 1,000 web map views, geocode requests, direction requests, and matrix elements per month for mobile SDKs and web apps. The free version also includes 5 GB of dataset storage for satellite and street maps, an unlimited amount of styles for Mapbox Studio, and access to create public and free web/mobile apps.

Now, it should be noted that there is a commercial option that is required when you have a paid web app or website that is free or subscription-based, a private web app or website with restricted access, or an app or website that tracks assets / monitors people or things. The commercial plan includes private or paid apps for up to 250 seats, asset tracking for up to 1,000 different assets, and turn-by-turn navigation apps for up to 50 seats. The cost is the same as the free plan in addition to $499 per month:

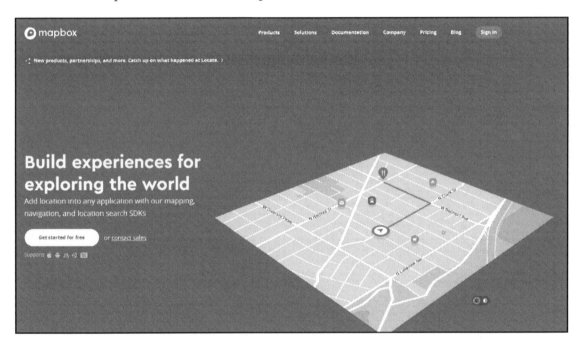

Project overview

We will be creating a small application that allows the user to select the location they want to walk to and it will set the destination. The build time will be around 20 minutes.

Getting started

The technical requirements for this application are as follows:

- Android device with kernel version 24 or above
- Unity 2018
- Mapbox (`https://www.mapbox.com/`)

Setting up Mapbox

We will now see how to set up Mapbox:

1. The very first thing we need to do is sign up for Mapbox. This requires a username, email address, and password:

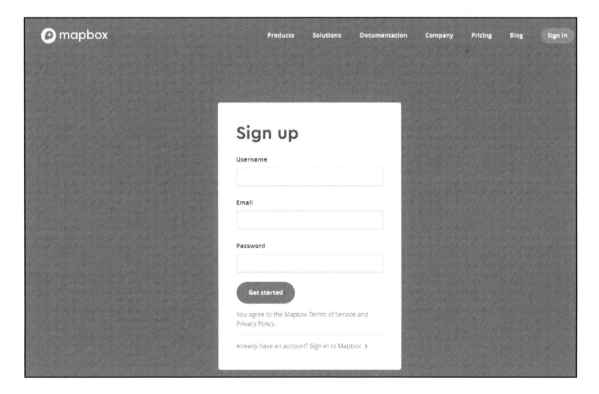

2. After you have signed up and verified your email address, it will take you to a page to find out which version of Mapbox you need. You have the option of **iOS**, **Android**, **Web**, and **Unity**:

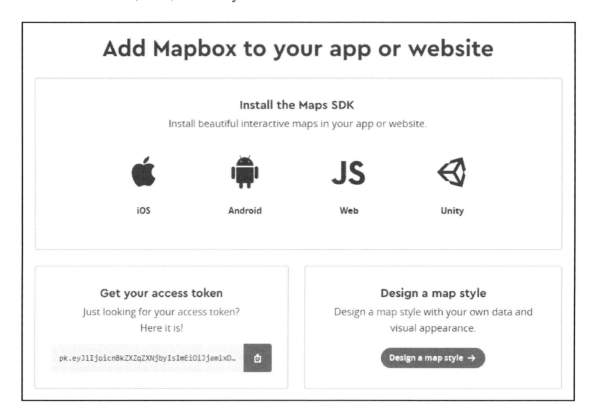

3. The version we want will obviously be the Maps SDK for Unity, so be sure to download the Unity package before proceeding:

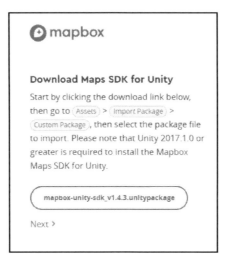

4. As per the following screenshot, you will be given an access token, which will be required to utilize the Mapbox software. Be sure to copy this key and paste it into Notepad for later use:

5. Create a new Unity project and call it `Chapter6` or `Fitness for Fun`:

6. Import the Mapbox Unity asset file into the project:

7. This will probably take some time to install:

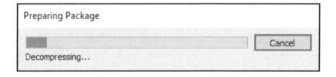

8. Right away, after the installation, you should notice a new menu item called **Mapbox**. This opens up quite a few new features that are exposed for us to play with:

9. **Mapbox** gives us **Atlas Template Generator**, **Clear File Cache**, **Setup**, and **Map Editor** options:

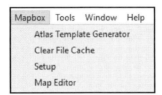

10. The **Mapbox Atlas Template Generator** is a tool that allows you to create and test custom map atlases:

For every item we look at in this section, exit from it immediately after taking a look at it so we can continue. We will revisit the items we need when building the project.

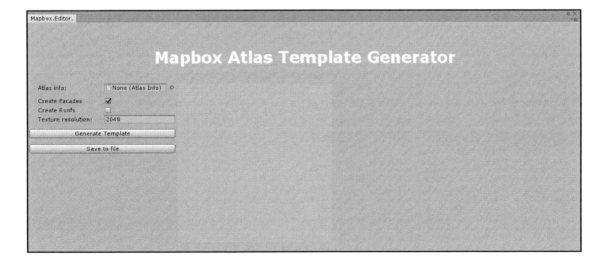

11. The **Map Editor** allows you to visualize the underlying data structure of the maps you create and use:

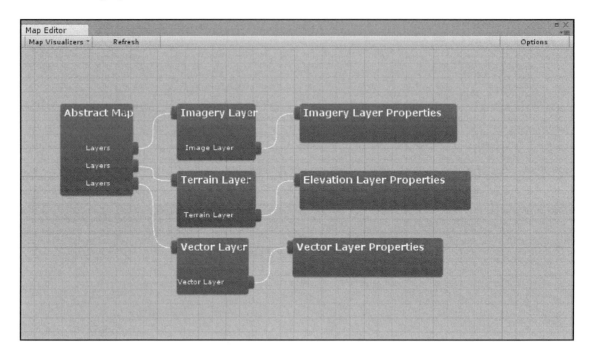

12. In addition to that, the Map Editor's data is tied directly to the Map object's **Abstract Map Script**. Any changes you make to the **Abstract Map Script** data is reflected in the **Map Editor**, and any changes you make in the **Map Editor** are reflected in the Abstract Map Script's data:

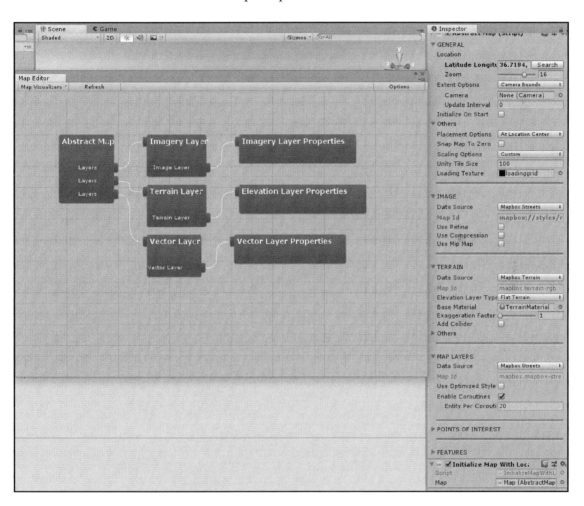

13. The **Mapbox Setup** option allows you to select **Example** scenes or **Map Prefabs**, however, this can only be accessed after you copy and paste your **Access Token** and submit the information. This will require you to be connected to the internet for verification:

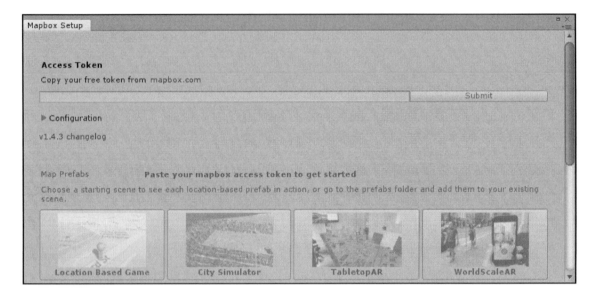

Important items to note

With different project types, you will have prefabs that will automatically be added to the active scene. In this section, we will go over the main object that is added to any template type, which is the Map object.

The Map is the most important object that is added to with any of our templates and has many extremely important items within the script that we should go over:

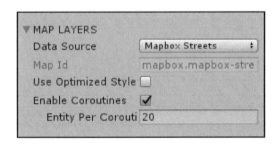

The first item within the Map object is the **Abstract Map** script. The most important items within are **MAP LAYERS**, **GENERAL**, **Location**, and **Others**:

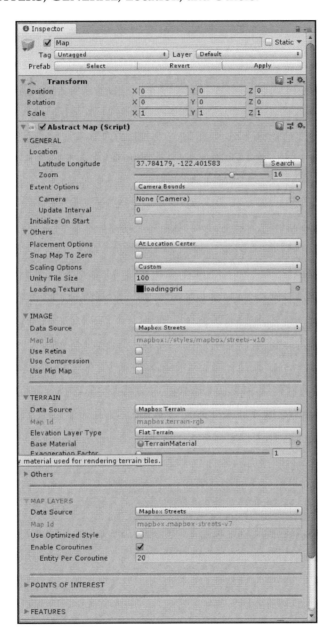

Within the **GENERAL** tab, we have:

- **Latitude Longitude**: If you click on **Search**, you can set this by typing in an address, or country and city, or even city and state, depending on the location you want to utilize. It will automatically convert it to be latitude and longitude values.
- **Zoom**: This is specifically set for how close and far away the map can be drawn; be advised that the zoom function will only work appropriately if you have the proper tilesets generated for it.
- **Extent Options**: These are how far you want the map to be drawn. By default, it is set to the bounds of the camera.
- **Camera**: This is the camera you want to use, whether it is an AR camera with Vuforia, ARCore, ARKit, or even the regular Unity camera.
- **Update Interval**: This is how long the program should wait before updating positions and drawing.
- **Initialize On Start**: This is a Boolean value for whether or not you want the map to immediately be drawn upon the start of the scene:

In the **Others** tab, we have a few options as well:

- **Placement Options** allows you to choose between **At Location Center** and **At Tile Center**. This controls the center or root placement of the tiles. Location center is able to be defined by you, whereas the tile center is the center of the tile.
- **Snap Map To Zero** is a Boolean value that specifies whether or not the map's root should be snapped to 0,0,0.

- **Scaling Options** allows you to choose whether you want a custom or world scale. **Custom** is defined by Unity using a Mercator conversion factor. **World scale** means that the actual scale is rendered and the Mercator conversion is ignored.
- **Unity Tile Size** is the size of the tiles used in Unity units.
- **Loading Texture** is the texture used when the textures are loading.

The next tab is the **IMAGE** tab:

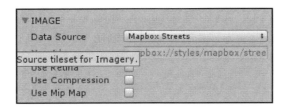

- **Data Source**: This is the source of our maps. We can use **Mapbox Streets**, **Mapbox Outdoors**, **Mapbox Dark**, **Mapbox Light**, **Mapbox Satellite**, **Mapbox Satellite Street**, **Custom**, or **None**. These are essentially theme options for the map you want to use.
- **Use Retina**: This is a Boolean that allows you to choose whether you want to enable the usage of larger texture maps and better visual quality for retina displays.
- **Use Compression**: This is a Boolean that allows you to choose to use Unity compression for the tile texture.
- **Use Mip Map**: This is a Boolean that lets you choose whether to use Unity-generated mip mapping.

The next tab is **TERRAIN**, which gives us the ability to modify the terrain of our Mapbox maps:

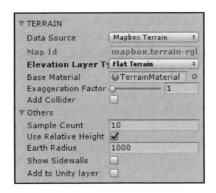

- **Data Source**: This is the first option available, and it lets us choose between using **Mapbox Terrain**, **Custom**, or **None**. **Mapbox Terrain** provides us with digital elevation with worldwide coverage. **Custom** allows us to use a custom elevation model. **None** is a flat terrain.
- **Map Id**: This is the Id of the corresponding tileset that we want to use.
- **Elevation Layer Type**: This gives us the choice between **Flat Terrain**, **Terrain with Elevation**, **Low Polygon Terrain**, and **Globe Terrain**. This allows us to render our terrain with the specified elevation type. **Flat Terrain** renders a flat terrain with no elevation. **Terrain with Elevation** renders terrain with elevation from the source specified. **Low Polygon Terrain** renders a low polygon terrain with elevation from the source specified. **Globe Terrain** renders a terrain with no elevation for a globe.
- **Base Material**: This is the material used to render the terrain tiles.
- **Exaggeration Factor**: This multiplies the factor to vertically exaggerate elevation on the terrain, however, it does not work with the **Flat Terrain Elevation Layer Type**.
- **Add Collider**: This is a Boolean that lets us add Unity physics colliders to terrain tiles for detecting collisions.

The **Others** tab within the **TERRAIN** tab has a few options available to us as well:

- **Sample Count**: This gives us the resolution for our terrain, with the result being an n x n grid.
- **Use Relative Height**: This is a Boolean that lets us use a world-relative scale for scaling the terrain height.
- **Earth Radius**: This is the radius of the Earth we want to use in Unity units of measurements, which is meters.
- **Show Sidewalls**: This is a Boolean that adds side walls to terrain meshes, which reduces visual artifacts.
- **Add to Unity layer**: This adds the terrain tiles to the Unity layer. Upon checking the checkbox, you will get the choice of which layer you want to add them to—**Default**, **TransparentFX**, **Ignore Raycast**, **Water**, **UI**, **Postprocessing**, and **Add Layer**.

Next is the **MAP LAYERS** tab:

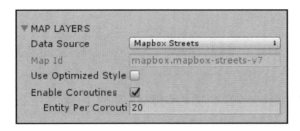

- **Data Source**: This is the source dataset for the vector data.
- **Map Id**: This is the Id of the map we are using.
- **Use Optimized Style**: This is a Boolean that allows us to use Mapbox-style-optimized tilesets that remove any layers or features in the tile that are not represented by a Mapbox style. Style-optimized vector tiles are smaller, serve over the wire, and are a great way to reduce the size of offline caches.
- **Enable Coroutines**: This is a Boolean that allows us to use coroutines.
- **Entity Per Coroutine**: This specifies how many entities can be grouped together in a single coroutine call.

POINTS OF INTEREST is the next tab. Here you can create special markers for important locations in your application or game:

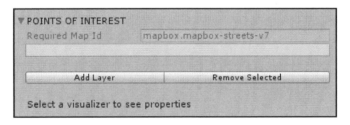

- **Required Map Id**: This is the map Id of the tileset we are using and cannot be empty.
- **Add Layer**: This allows us to add points of interest layers.
- **Remove Selected**: This allows us to delete a layer.

The last tab is **FEATURES**, which gives us **Vector Layer Visualizers** with the options to add or remove visualizers. **FEATURES** allow us to modify how certain features look in relation to the point of interest we create:

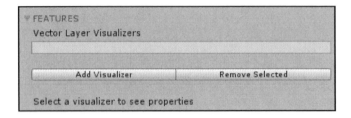

- **Add Visualizer**: This allows us to change how we visualize a points of interest layer
- **Remove Selected**: This allows us to delete the selected visualizer

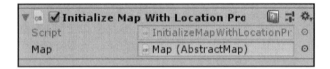

Finally, we have another script, called **Initialize Map With Location Provider**, which only has the option to add an **Abstract Map object** to it. This script does what the name states—it registers if you are on an iOS, Windows, or Android device, and selects the **Location Provider** that is most relevant for it.

Setting up the project

It's now time to set up our project:

1. Let's create a new scene and call it `FitnessFun`:

2. Click on **Mapbox** and then **Setup**. This will open a setup menu where you need to paste your **Access Token** in order to gain access to the **Map Prefabs** template:

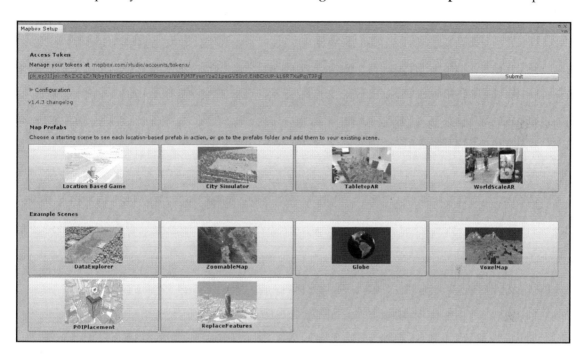

3. The **Map Prefabs** template we want to use is **Location Based Game**:

4. It will add a prefab onto our scene, which will have what looks like a pawn in the scene edit tab:

5. If you look over in the **Hierarchy** pane, you will notice a LocationBasedGame prefab added there, and if you drill down to look at the objects inside, you will see a **Map**, **Player**, and **LocationProvider** inside. You will also notice a **Canvas** and **EventSystem** automatically added to the **Hierarchy**:

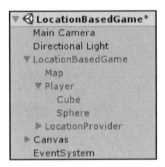

6. Inside the `Scenes` folder, create a `Scripts` folder:

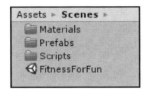

7. Inside that `Scripts` folder, create a C# script called `TargetLocationController`:

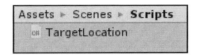

8. Create another script called `DestroyTargetLocation`:

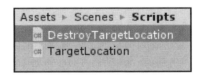

9. Go back to the **Hierarchy** pane and make a copy of the **Player** component:

10. Remove the **Immediate Position** and **Rotation with Location** scripts along with renaming it to `targetLocation`:

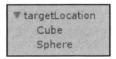

11. Inside the `Scenes` folder, create a folder called `Prefabs`:

12. Drag and drop the `TargetLocation` object into the `Prefabs` folder:

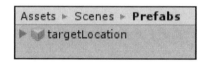

13. Navigate to our `Scripts` folder and open the **TargetLocationController** script.

We need to write our script to create a new instance of the `TargetLocation` object and to destroy the object when something happens.

Scripting the project

In this section, we'll see how to script our project:

1. We will first make sure to utilize Unity Engine, as we need access to `MonoBehaviour`:

   ```
   using UnityEngine;
   ```

2. Our public class will be called `TargetLocationController`, which is the same name as the script file we named in the Unity Editor. We will also inherit from `MonoBehaviour`:

   ```
   public class TargetLocationController : MonoBehaviour
   {
   ```

3. We will create a public `GameObject` called `targetObject`; this is so that we can drag and drop our prefab onto this object to set a reference to it:

   ```
   private GameObject targetObject;
   ```

4. We will create a `Start()` method at this point. We want to find the object in the project with the tag of `targetLocation`, as we will be creating it upon a touch event instantiating it:

```
private void Start()
{
    targetObject =
GameObject.FindGameObjectWithTag("targetLocation");
}
```

5. We will need to create a `SetLocation` method and instantiate a new raycast to utilize the touch event the way we want for reading finger presses on the screen:

```
private void SetLocation()
{
RaycastHit hit = new RaycastHit();
```

6. We need to loop through to check on our input via touch events:

```
for (int i = 0; i < Input.touchCount; ++i)
```

7. We check to see if the touch count is greater than 0, and if our touch phase is moved:

```
if (Input.touchCount > 0 && Input.GetTouch(0).phase ==
TouchPhase.Moved)
{
```

8. Now, we will construct a ray from the current touch coordinates on the screen:

```
Ray ray = Camera.main.ScreenPointToRay(Input.GetTouch(i).position);
```

9. We need to do a check to see if the raycast hits anything:

```
if (Physics.Raycast(ray, out hit))
```

10. If the raycast hits anything, then we will create a new instance of our prefab with the position based on our touch event:

```
Instantiate(targetObject, new Vector3(Input.GetTouch(i).position.x,
4.23f, Input.GetTouch(i).position.y), Quaternion.identity);
}
}
```

11. In our `Update()` method, we call our `SetLocation` script:

```
private void Update()
{
SetLocation();
}
}
```

12. Now, we just need a simple collision check script to check if the player object collides with the `targetlocation` object. We want to destroy our `targetLocation` object if the player object collides with it.

13. Open the `Destroy Target Location` script.

14. We will need the `UnityEngine` namespace as usual, since we want to inherit from `MonoBehaviour`:

```
using UnityEngine;
 using System.Collections;
```

15. The name of the class is the same as the name we gave the C# script file and inherits from `MonoBehaviour`, so we can attach it to a game object in the Unity Editor:

```
public class DestroyTargetLocation: MonoBehaviour
 {
```

16. We create an `OnCollisionEnter` method with the parameters of `Collision col`:

```
void OnCollisionEnter (Collision col)
 {
```

17. We will do a simple `if` check to see if what we are colliding with is the `targetLocation` object via the object's tag name:

```
if(col.gameObject.tag == "targetLocation")
 {
```

18. If the simple `if` check returns true, then we will destroy the `targetLocation` object:

```
Destroy(col.gameObject);
 }
 }
 }
```

We have everything we need to finalize the project.

Finalizing the project

We will now finalize our project:

1. Navigate back to the Unity Editor, attach the `targetLocation` script to the player object, and set the object to be the `targetLocation` object:

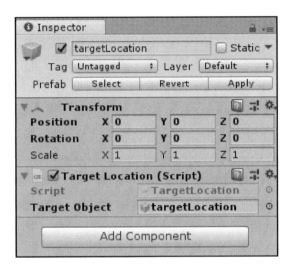

2. Attach the `DestroyTargetLocation` script to our object called `LocationBasedGame`:

3. Now we can click on **File** | **Build**:

4. Set the project type for **Android**:

5. Make sure the only scene added for building is the `Chapter6` scene. If the scenes list is empty, click on **Add Current Scene**:

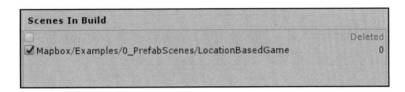

6. Now, build the project and install it on your Android device to run the program.

Summary

In this chapter, we conceptualized and created a fitness application prototype that encourages walking to different locations for the user's enjoyment. We learned about Mapbox and what it does, and we learned how to integrate it into Unity. We then leveraged Mapbox to create a viewable AR map that is able to use geolocation technology to track the user's position and destination.

In the next chapter, we will go over creating an application/game that facilitates learning for children by creating a picture puzzle.

Questions

Leverage Vuforia, ARCore, or ARKit to be able to read certain objects in the world to save where you have gone or to gameify this application. To do this, you will need to create AR markers, which are heavily documented with many examples online on how to leverage them for different project types.

1. You can use Mapbox with ARCore, ARKit, and Vuforia:

   A.) True
   B.) False

2. Mapbox is completely free:

    A.) True
    B.) False

3. Mapbox is fully integrated to work with Unity:

    A.) True
    B.) False

4. Mapbox has web-based software to create custom maps:

    A.) True
    B.) False

5. Mapbox has an example scene prebuilt that allows you to use UnityChan as your player model:

    A.) True
    B.) False

Further reading

Mapbox is heavily documented for Unity, iOS, Android, React Native, and QT. They have tutorials on how to work with Mapbox Studio, how to directly leverage their Maps, Directions, and Geocoding APIs. The quickest way to access their documentation is to go to `https://www.mapbox.com/developers/`.

7
Snap it! Adding Filters to Pictures

In this chapter, we will create an application that will allow us to add an overlay over a person's head. If this application sounds familiar, that is because there are many applications that are on the market that do just this, and today, you will learn how to do so as well.

In this chapter, you will learn about the following:

- OpenCV
- Setting up OpenCV
- Incorporating OpenCV into Unity
- Creating a prototype project using OpenCV and Unity

Project overview

This project makes heavy use of facial recognition-and-detection algorithms, which requires knowledge of OpenCV.

Build time: two hours

Getting started

In this section, we will cover a few things that you will need and some optional items for more in depth building from source requirements.

- OpenCV 3.4.1, which you can find at `https://opencv.org/releases.html`, is the library itself in pure source form or in library form. If you want the Unity specific plugin, you can purchase it from `https://assetstore.unity.com/packages/tools/integration/opencv-for-unity-21088`, along with the sister library file at `https://enoxsoftware.com/dlibfacelandmarkdetector/`.
- Unity 2018 can be download from `https://store.unity.com/`.
- Visual Studio, a requirement for writing or compiling source code, can be downloaded from `https://visualstudio.microsoft.com/downloads/`.
- CMake, which you can download from `https://CMake.org/download/`, is required when building your own version of the library, the plugin, and the source for OpenCV.
- Python, which is a requirement if you need to build your own library for OpenCV, can be downloaded from `https://www.python.org/getit/`.

What is OpenCV?

OpenCV stands for **Open Computer Vision**. OpenCV is an open source computer vision and machine learning software library that was built with C++ and has C++, Python, Java, and Matlab interfaces to support Windows, Linux, Android, and macOS.

OpenCV mainly focuses on real-time vision applications, although it can be used for machine learning very nicely. The library has many optimized algorithms and functions to compose or support such algorithms for state-of-the-art computer vision and machine learning, with roughly 2,500. To break down the ratio here, there are roughly 500 algorithms, and the rest are functions to compose or support these algorithms.

Talking about algorithms is fun and all, but I'm sure you are more interested in knowing what these algorithms are capable of doing. The algorithms are designed to be used to detect faces, recognize faces, identify objects, detect and classify human actions in video feeds, track camera movements, move object tracking, extraction of 3D models from objects, produce point clouds from stereo cameras in 3D, stitch images together for high resolution images, quickly find the same or similar images from an image database, red-eye removal, eye tracking, detect scenery, and establish markers for augmented reality overlay, and so much more.

OpenCV can work with TensorFlow, Caffe, Torch, Yolo, Vuforia, ARCore, and ARKit with ease. OpenCV can be used for **Augmented Reality (AR)**, **Virtual Reality (VR)**, and **Mixed Reality (MR)**. You can use visual scripting options, such as PlayMaker, and have access to all methods available in OpenCV. OpenCV also works with tons of different hardware, such as HoloLens, Oculus Rift, Telepathy, Kinect, and Raspberry Pi, to name a few.

We have two different options for gaining access to OpenCV. The first one is to build from source and create our own wrappers to create a Unity plugin for OpenCV. The second option is to purchase OpenCV for Unity from the Unity Asset Store.

If you want to go the easy route and purchase the Unity extension, it will cost 70 dollars, unless you have a Unity Plus/Pro membership, which will decrease the cost to 56 dollars. The good news is that it supports Unity Version 5.6 or greater and is based on OpenCV 3.4.1.

There are sample assets packs that you can download from the Unity Asset Store or from GitHub that will give you prebuilt examples for working with HoloLens Face Detection Overlay, FaceLandmark Detection, Facemasking, Real-time Face Recognition, Markerless AR. Face Swapping, Kinect with OpenCV, Facetracking, working with Vuforia and OpenCV, and marker-based AR.

Now, the other option, in other words, the cheap route, because, let's be honest, the Unity plugin is rather pricey, especially for younger developers or those who just want to try out OpenCV to see whether it is a good fit, is to build from source. What benefits do we gain from build from source, besides the low cost?

We get to decide which aspects of the library we need, for one. This is a huge bonus, as we can remove bloat to reduce the file and compile size. However, even when doing this, you can have the same features, or even more than the Unity plugin, since you are building from source.

The downside is that there are many things you need to get the full compilation of the source taken care of, which is dependent on whether you want to use prebuilt binaries or building your own library from scratch.

To build from scratch, you will need Visual Studio with C++ modules installed, CMake, Python Version 2.7 or later, Numpy, **Intel Threading Building Blocks (TBB)**, **Intel Integrated Performance Primitives (IPP)**, Intel IPP Asynchronous C/C++, Eigen, CUDA Toolkit, OpenEXR, OpenNI Framework, and Doxygen.

Creating the project with paid assets

In this section, we will use the Unity asset files, as they are a bit shorter to set up. The Dlib FaceLandmark Detector costs 40 dollars, and OpenCV for Unity costs 70 dollars. That means to build this project, you will need to have spent 110 dollars. Sadly, there are no free alternatives in the Unity Asset store, and if you want to build the project without purchasing the assets, you will need to build the wrappers and implementations on your own. Now, follow these steps:

1. Create a brand new Unity Project. I will call mine Snap:

2. Make sure your Assets directory is completely empty:

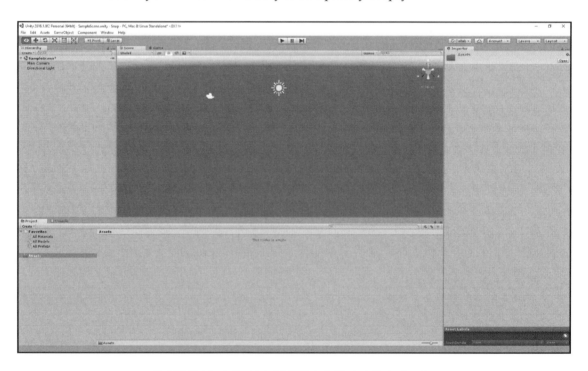

The text in this screenshot is not important. It indicates that the Assets directory is empty.

3. We will start by importing OpenCV into Unity. This will take some time to complete:

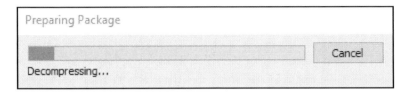

4. You will have many examples that include some very nice shaders that can be used in other projects, so import everything:

5. Your `Assets` directory should have an `OpenCVForUnity` and a `Realistic_Water_Fountain` folder:

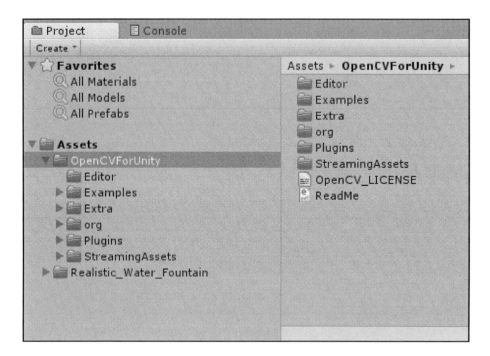

6. Now, we will need to import the Dlib Facelandmark Detector.
7. The last asset we will need is the **FaceMask Example**. Click on this link: `https://assetstore.unity.com/packages/templates/tutorials/facemask-example-79999`.
8. This package contains some additional scripts, as well as some examples of how to apply face masking to the camera, to be able to record videos or take a picture.
9. Use the **FaceMask Example** scene, and this will create our basic prototype.

We now have a working prototype for Snap it. You can add more features such as different items to cover the face, cover only a small portion of the head, add shader effects to the scene, and so much more to create your own feature-rich AR application based on OpenCV and the Dlib Facelandmark Detector.

Installing and building OpenCV

Now, what if you don't have the funds to build this project with paid assets that would make your life easier? Well, the option is to build from scratch. It is much more involved and is generally a rabbit hole that more experienced developers tend to go down than beginners.

This isn't to say that beginners can't follow along and build from scratch themselves; in fact, I suggest that if you are a beginner, follow along, as there are many new things to learn from this exercise, from dealing with other people's source files, to incorporating them into your own projects with an understanding of that code base.

To get OpenCV set up to run with Unity, we have a few steps we need to go through. We need to download OpenCV and CMake. OpenCV is the library we will be heavily utilizing, and CMake is the software that allows us to manage the build process in any given operating system and compiler with independence in mind.

Downloading OpenCV

Let's get started by first downloading OpenCV. We could go down the route of getting the pure source files or by getting the prebuilt binaries, both of which have their own pros and cons associated with them. For example, the pure source files version would require us to have every library used within OpenCV and language associated installed and configured to be able to build our own binaries. We will simplify the process just a hair, by going with the prebuilt binaries approach. Follow these steps:

1. To get started with building OpenCV from prebuilt binaries, we first need to download the files we need. There are two possibilities for this, `https://opencv.org/opencv-3-3.html` or `https://sourceforge.net/projects/opencvlibrary/`:

2. We need to choose the installation version we want; in this case, I am going to go with the latest version, which is 3.4.1, as it is the same as the Unity extension version:

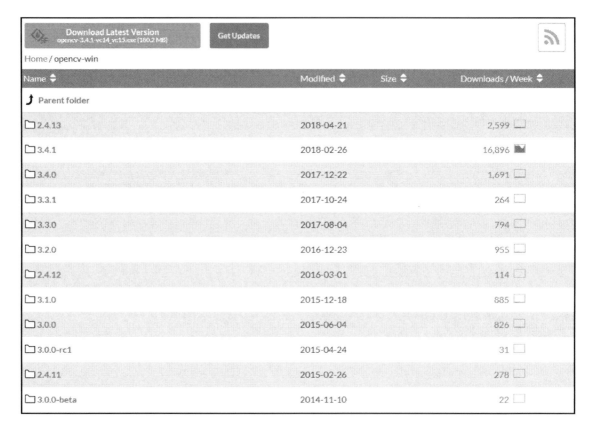

3. The executable file is 172 MB in size, so, depending on your internet connection speeds, you could have a long download time:

4. Create a new folder to house the extracted OpenCV files:

5. Now, we have our OpenCV self-extracting file:

6. Right-click on the installer file, and select **Run as administrator**. We need to have elevated privileges to make sure the project extracts correctly:

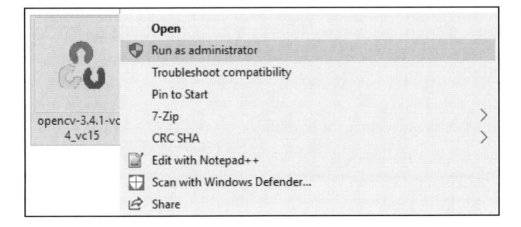

7. Select the folder you created as the installation location:

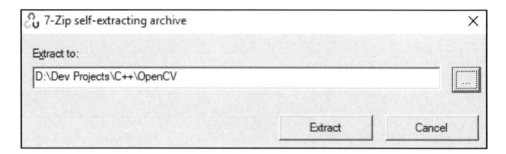

8. Extracting the files should not take long:

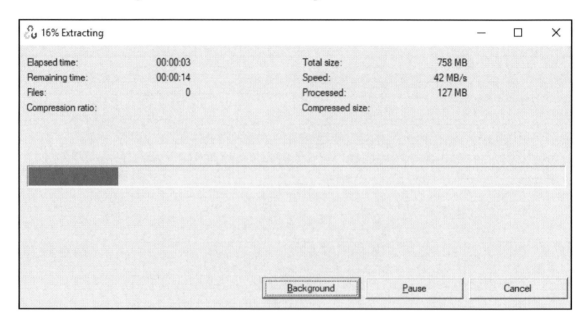

9. Now, we have extracted OpenCV.

Downloading CMake

Now that OpenCV has been download, it is time to do the same for CMake, as both of these files are integral to continuing properly.

This is only the case if you decided to go with the source direction instead of the binaries method, so I will touch on these steps a little as well.

Downloading CMake is a rather quick and painless process, regardless of whether you are using Linux, macOS, or Windows. Since I want to build with Windows, I will showcase the steps with that particular OS in mind.

1. Go to `CMake.org`; click on download latest, and scroll down to latest release to download CMake:

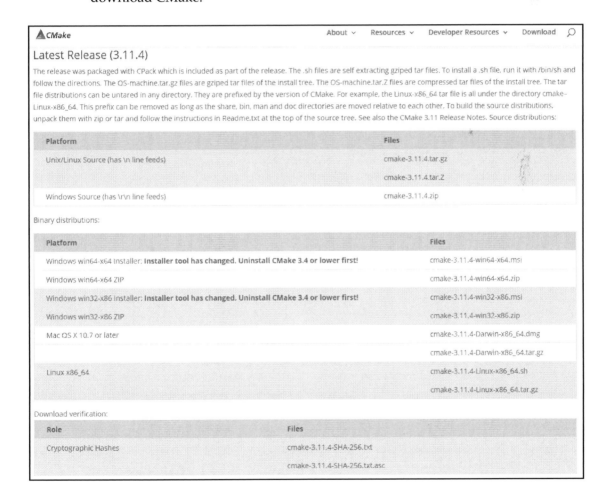

2. Double-click on CMake to run the setup wizard:

3. Put a check mark in the *License Agreement* block and click **Next**:

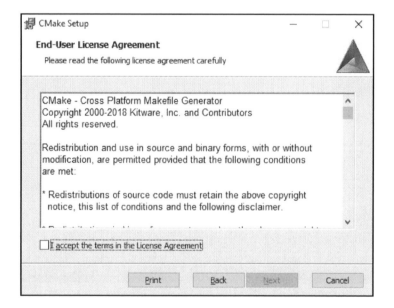

4. Make sure to **Add CMake to the system PATH for current or all users**, depending on your preference. Just make sure that it is set to the system path before clicking **Next:**

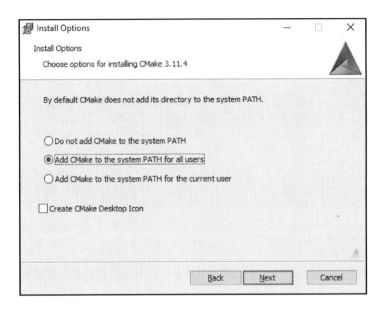

5. Click **Next** to install CMake to whatever folder you want:

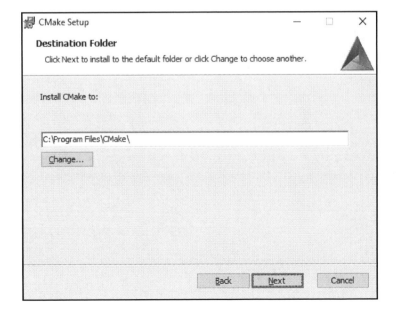

6. To install CMake, it requires elevated privilges, so if you have UAC enabled and don't have admin rights, make sure you have someone nearby that can give you access to install:

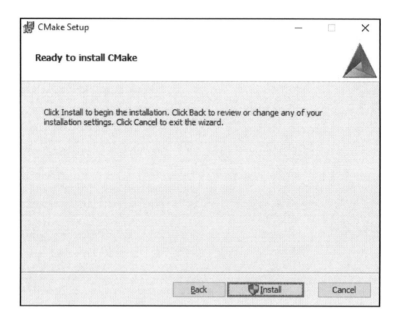

7. Installation will take a few minutes to complete:

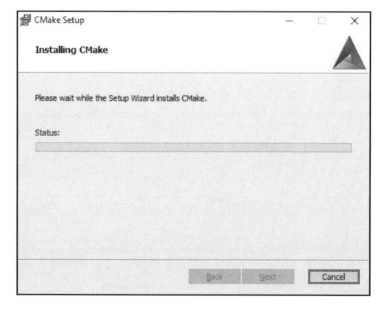

8. Click **Finish** to complete the installation process:

Configuring the CMake and OpenCV source files

Now, we can move on to configuring CMake and getting everything set up to build OpenCV as a library to utilize within Unity. Now, to do this, you need the full-on source code of OpenCV, instead of the binaries, which you can grab from `https://github.com/opencv/opencv/archive/3.3.0.zip.` or `https://github.com/opencv/opencv/archive/3.3.0.zip.`

Start *CMake* (`CMake-gui`). You may again enter it in the start menu search or get it from **All Programs | CMake 2.8 | CMake** (`CMake-gui`). First, select the directory for the source files of the OpenCV library (1). Then, specify a directory where you will build the binary files for OpenCV library (2).

Press the **Configure** button to specify the compiler (and the IDE) you want to use. Note that you can choose between different compilers for making either 64 bit or 32 bit libraries. Select the one you use in your application development.

CMake will start based on your system variables and will try to automatically locate as many packages as possible. You can modify the packages to use for the build in the *WITH* ‣ *WITH_X* menu points (where *X* is the package abbreviation).

Select all the packages you want to use, and again press the **Configure** button. For an easier overview of the build options, make sure the **Grouped** option under the binary directory selection is turned on. For some of the packages, CMake may not find all of the required files or directories. If it doesn't find all of them, CMake will throw an error in its output window (located at the bottom of the GUI) and set its field values to not-found constants.

Press the **Configure** button again and ensure that no errors are reported. CMake will create the project files by pushing the **Generate** button. Go to the build directory and open the created OpenCV solution. Depending on just how many options you have selected, the solution may contain quite a lot of projects, so be tolerant on the IDE at the startup. Now, you need to build both the **Release** and the **Debug** binaries. Use the drop-down menu on your IDE to change to another of these after building for one of them.

In the end, you can observe the built binary files inside the bin directory.

To collect the header and the binary files, which you will use during your own projects, into a separate directory (similarly to how the pre-built binaries ship), you need to explicitly build the **Install** project.

To test your build, just go into the Build/bin/Debug or the Build/bin/Release directory and start a couple of applications, such as `contours.exe`. If they run, you are done.

For more in-depth information on this, go to `https://docs.opencv.org/3.0-beta/doc/tutorials/introduction/windows_install/windows_install.html`. The OpenCV documentation will go into this in more detail, along with the other tools you will need to install to go down this route.

OpenCV with Unity

We can now move on to importing our dlls into Unity and writing our wrapper classes to handle interfacing with OpenCV and Unity. That way, we can then create our scripts to build our project:

1. Create a folder. I will call mine `ConfigureOpenCV`:

2. We need to create a new empty C++ project in Visual Studio. I will call mine `ConfigureOpenCV`, with the location being set in the `ConfigureOpenCV` folder:

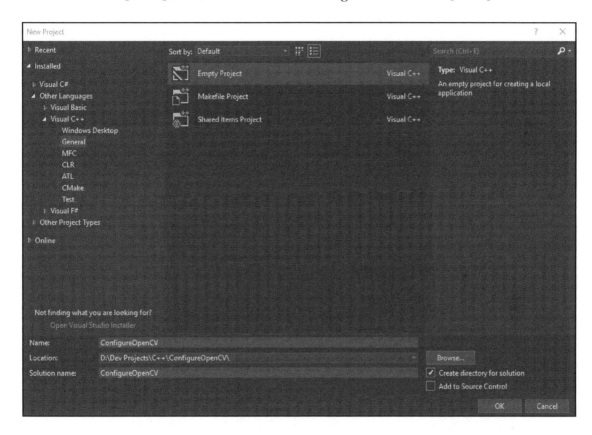

3. Set the platform to be **x64** in Visual Studio:

4. Right-click on the project properties file and select **Properties**:

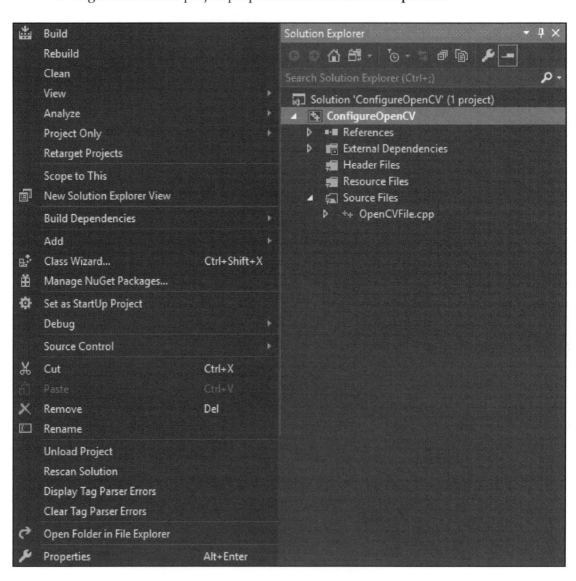

5. This will open our properties window:

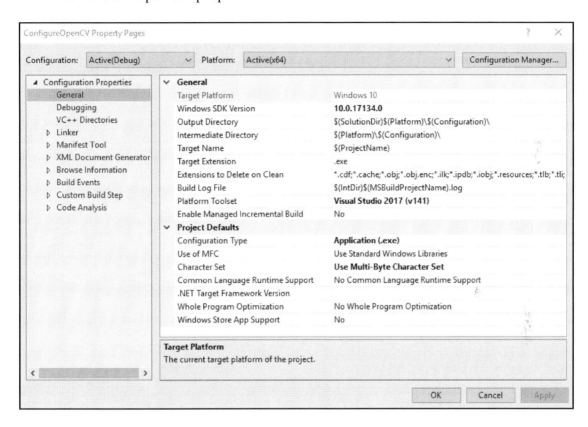

6. The first thing we need to do is change **Target Extension** in the **General** tab from .exe to .dll:

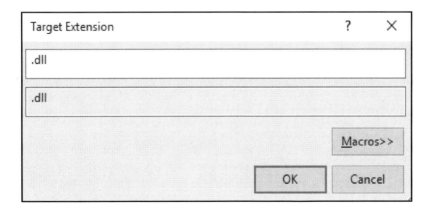

7. We need to change the **Configuration Type** from **Application (.exe)** to **Dynamic Library (.dll)**:

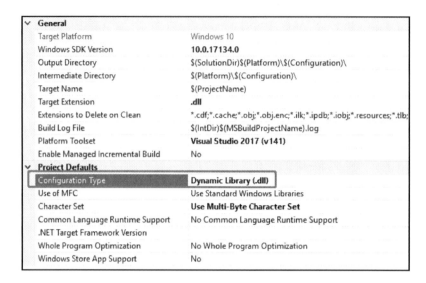

8. Over in **VC++ Directories**, add our OPENCV_DIRs to include it in **Include Directories**:

9. Over in Linker's **General** Tab, add `$(OPENCV_DIR)\lib\Debug` to the **Additional Library Directories** option:

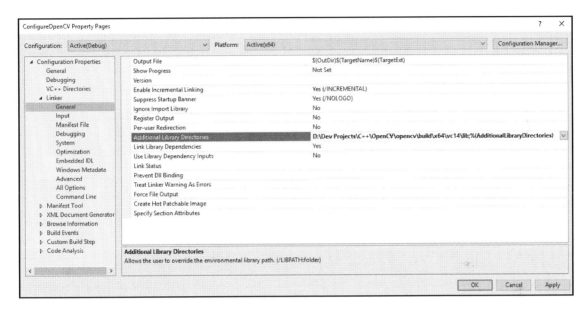

10. Finally, in the Linker's **Input** tab, we need to add a few items to the **Additional Dependencies** option. Those items will be the following:

- `opencv_core310.lib` (or `opencv_world330.lib`, depending on your OpenCV version)
- `opencv_highgui310.lib`
- `opencv_objdetect310.lib`
- `opencv_videoio310.lib`
- `opencv_imgproc310.lib`

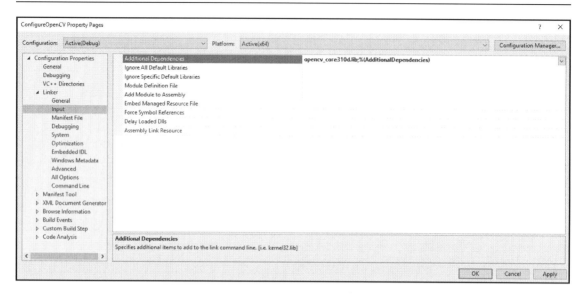

Figure shows the location of Additional Dependencies in the Linker's Input tab with opencv_core added.

11. Now, we can create a new CPP file:

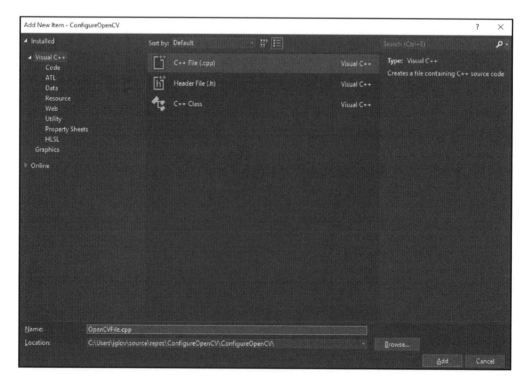

We will now incorporate the headers and namespaces we absolutely need here:

```
#include "opencv2/objdetect.hpp"
#include "opencv2/highgui.hpp"
#include "opencv2/imgproc.hpp"
#include <iostream>
#include <stdio.h>
using namespace std;
using namespace cv;
```

1. Declare a `struct` that will be used to pass data from C++ to Mono:

```
struct Circle
{
Circle(int x, int y, int radius) : X(x), Y(y), Radius(radius) {}
int X, Y, Radius;
};
```

2. `CascadeClassifer` is a class used for object detection:

```
CascadeClassifier _faceCascade;
```

3. Create a string that will serve as the name of the window:

```
String _windowName = "OpenCV";
```

4. Video Capture is a class used to open a video file, or capture a device or an IP video stream for video capture:

```
VideoCapture _capture;
```

5. Create an integer value to store the scale:

```
int _scale = 1;
```

6. `extern "C"`, as a refresher, will avoid name mangling from C++. Our first method is `Init` for initialization:

```
extern "C" int __declspec(dllexport) __stdcall  Init(int&
outCameraWidth, int& outCameraHeight)
{
```

7. We will create an `if` statement to load the LBP face `cascade.xml` file that is part of `CVFeatureParams`; if it cannot load, then it will exit with a return code of −1:

```
if (!_faceCascade.load("lbpcascade_frontalface.xml"))
return -1;
```

8. Now, we will open the video capture stream:

```
_capture.open(0);
```

9. If the video stream is not opened, then we will exit with a return code of −2:

```
if (!_capture.isOpened())
return -2;
```

10. We will set the camera width:

```
outCameraWidth = _capture.get(CAP_PROP_FRAME_WIDTH);
```

11. And we also need to set the camera height:

```
outCameraHeight = _capture.get(CAP_PROP_FRAME_HEIGHT);
return 0;
}
```

12. Now, we need to make sure that we create a method to close the capture stream and release the video capture device:

```
extern "C" void __declspec(dllexport) __stdcall  Close()
{
_capture.release();
}
```

13. The next step is to create a method that sets the video scale:

```
extern "C" void __declspec(dllexport) __stdcall SetScale(int scale)
{
_scale = scale;
}
```

14. Next up, we will create a method that allows us to detect an object:

```
extern "C" void __declspec(dllexport) __stdcall Detect(Circle*
outFaces, int maxOutFacesCount, int& outDetectedFacesCount)
{
Mat frame;
_capture >> frame;
```

15. Next up, if the frame is empty, we need to guard against possible errors from this by exiting from the method:

```
if (frame.empty())
return;
```

16. Create a vector called `faces`:

```
std::vector<Rect> faces;
```

17. We will create **Mat**, which is one of the various constructors that forms a matrix with the name of `grayscaleFrame`:

```
Mat grayscaleFrame;
```

18. We then need to convert the frame to grayscale from RGB colorspace for proper cascade detection:

```
cvtColor(frame, grayscaleFrame, COLOR_BGR2GRAY);
Mat resizedGray;
```

19. The next step is to scale down for better performance:

```
resize(grayscaleFrame, resizedGray, Size(frame.cols / _scale,
frame.rows / _scale));
equalizeHist(resizedGray, resizedGray);
```

20. Next up, we will detect the `faces`:

```
_faceCascade.detectMultiScale(resizedGray, faces);
```

21. We will now create a for loop to draw the faces:

```
for (size_t i = 0; i < faces.size(); i++)
{
Point center(_scale * (faces[i].x + faces[i].width / 2), _scale *
(faces[i].y + faces[i].height / 2));
ellipse(frame, center, Size(_scale * faces[i].width / 2, _scale *
faces[i].height / 2), 0, 0, 360, Scalar(0, 0, 255), 4, 8, 0);
```

22. Now, we will send this information to the application:

```
outFaces[i] = Circle(faces[i].x, faces[i].y, faces[i].width / 2);
outDetectedFacesCount++;
```

23. Since we have a matrix, we need to make sure that we don't exceed the limits of the array. To do this, we will break if the faces count is equal to the max amount of faces count we have allocated; if it is, exit from the loop:

```
if (outDetectedFacesCount == maxOutFacesCount)
break;
}
```

24. The last thing we need to do is display the debug output:

```
imshow(_windowName, frame);
```

25. Now, build the `dll` file, and we can now begin to work in Unity.

OpenCV and Unity

Now, we can finally start working in Unity in this section. This is the easier part, where we just need to create our wrapper and our `MonoBehaviour` script to attach to an object.

Navigate to the `dll` file that we created. This should be in the **x64 | Debug** folder of the source project:

This PC › Local Disk (C:) › Users › jglov › source › repos › ConfigureOpenCV › x64 › Debug			
Name	Date modified	Type	Size
ConfigureOpenCV.dll	7/20/2018 1:01 PM	Application extens	94 KB
ConfigureOpenCV.exp	7/20/2018 1:01 PM	Exports Library File	2 KB
ConfigureOpenCV.ilk	7/20/2018 1:01 PM	Incremental Linke...	465 KB
ConfigureOpenCV.lib	7/20/2018 12:57 PM	Object File Library	3 KB
ConfigureOpenCV.pdb	7/20/2018 1:01 PM	Program Debug D...	532 KB

Create two folder called `Plugins` and `Scripts` in Unity, just as we did in `Chapter3`.

Now, we will create two scripts. One for our `Wrapper` class, and the other for our `MonoBehaviour`. The `Wrapper` class will be called `OpenCVWrapper`, and the `MonoBehaviour` class will be called `OpenCVFaceDetection`.

Open the `OpenCVWrapper` class in Visual Studio. It is time to write some more code.

We only need to use the `InteropServices` namespace for this class:

```
using System.Runtime.InteropServices;
```

We will create an `internal static class` this time around:

```
internal static class OpenCVWrapper
{
```

We will import the `Init` function that we created in the last step, and we need to make sure that we reference the parameters. The `ref` keyword is very similar to the `&` keyword in C++:

```
[DllImport("UnityOpenCVSample")]
internal static extern int Init(ref int outCameraWidth, ref int
outCameraHeight);
```

We will import the `Close` function, which closes the connection and will avoid memory leaks when we use the functions that we've created:

```
[DllImport("UnityOpenCVSample")]
internal static extern int Close();
```

We will import the `SetScale` function we created, along with keeping the parameters that we required in C++:

```
[DllImport("UnityOpenCVSample")]
internal static extern int SetScale(int downscale);
```

We will import the `Detect` function, and this one is a bit different, as we are actually using a pointer; this will be very important very soon, as this deals with unsafe code in C# and Unity. If you aren't familiar, the `*` keyword denotes a pointer, which is the address of the object in memory:

```
[DllImport("UnityOpenCVSample")]
internal unsafe static extern void Detect(CvCircle* outFaces, int
maxOutFacesCount, ref int outDetectedFacesCount);
}
```

Lastly, we will create a structure that needs to be sequential and with the correct byte size (3 ints = 4 bytes * 3 = 12 bytes) for CvCircle:

```
[StructLayout(LayoutKind.Sequential, Size = 12)]
public struct CvCircle
{
public int X, Y, Radius;
}
```

This takes care of the wrapper class, and we can now move over to our `MonoBehaviour` class.

We need a few namespaces, as they will be fully utilized in this script:

```
using UnityEngine;
using System.Collections;
using System.Collections.Generic;
```

We have our class named the same as the file in the Unity Editor and inherit from `MonoBehaviour`:

```
public class OpenCVFaceDetection : MonoBehaviour
{
```

The main thing to notice here is that I have a reference to the camera and a `WebCamTexture`. This is because we will feed the data from the webcam to the camera:

```
public Camera camera;
public static List<Vector2> NormalizedFacePositions { get; private set; }
public static Vector2 CameraResolution;
private const int DetectionDownScale = 1;
private bool _ready;
private int _maxFaceDetectCount = 5;
private CvCircle[] _faces;
private Quaternion baseRotation;
private WebCamTexture webCamTexture;
```

In this `Start` method, we get everything set up and running. We also check to make sure that the `cascades.xml` file is able to be found (more on that in the next section):

```
void Start()
{
int camWidth = 0, camHeight = 0;
webCamTexture = new WebCamTexture();
Renderer renderer = GetComponent<Renderer>();
renderer.material.mainTexture = webCamTexture;
baseRotation = transform.rotation;
webCamTexture.Play();
camWidth = webCamTexture.width;
camHeight = webCamTexture.height;
int result = OpenCVWrapper.Init(ref camWidth, ref camHeight);
if (result < 0)
{
if (result == -1)
{
Debug.LogWarningFormat("[{0}] Failed to find cascades definition.",
GetType());
}
else if (result == -2)
{
Debug.LogWarningFormat("[{0}] Failed to open camera stream.", GetType());
}
return;
}
CameraResolution = new Vector2(camWidth, camHeight);
_faces = new CvCircle[_maxFaceDetectCount];
```

```
NormalizedFacePositions = new List<Vector2>();
OpenCVWrapper.SetScale(DetectionDownScale);
_ready = true;
}
```

This method will make sure that the connections are closed to the webcam. This will free up the resources and make sure that we don't leak any memory:

```
void OnApplicationQuit()
{
if (_ready)
{
OpenCVWrapper.Close();
}
}
```

This Update method makes sure that the orientation of the webcam is corrected, checks whether the camera is read or not, and actively tracks for face detection:

```
void Update()
{
if (!_ready)
{
return;
}
transform.rotation = baseRotation *
Quaternion.AngleAxis(webCamTexture.videoRotationAngle, Vector3.up);

int detectedFaceCount = 0;
unsafe
{
fixed (CvCircle* outFaces = _faces)
{
OpenCVWrapper.Detect(outFaces, _maxFaceDetectCount, ref
detectedFaceCount);
}
}

NormalizedFacePositions.Clear();
for (int i = 0; i < detectedFaceCount; i++)
{
NormalizedFacePositions.Add(new Vector2((_faces[i].X * DetectionDownScale)
/ CameraResolution.x, 1f - ((_faces[i].Y * DetectionDownScale) /
CameraResolution.y)));
}
}
}
```

Save the script and go back to the Unity Editor. You will immediately notice that Unity will show an error along the lines of *unsafe code needs to be allowed*. Let's go ahead and enable this feature. To do this, go to your **Player Settings**, which is located inside the **Build Settings.**

Inside the **Player Settings**, look down at the configuration inside **Other Settings**, and there is a checkbox called **Allow 'unsafe' Code**. Make sure that it is checked:

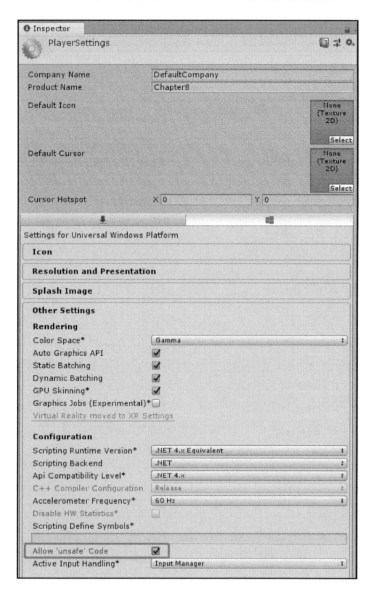

In the `Scripts` folder, you need one more file to be added; in my example file that you can download, I have quite a few more `.xml` files than what I am going to tell you to add. The reason for this is to allow you to play around with the different `.xml` files to see their results. You will have to update the C++ plugin to account for the proper `.xml` file you want to use; alternatively, you can update the `Init` function to take a string parameter to be able to change the `.xml` file in the Unity Editor.

In your `OpenCV` folder, navigate to `OpenCV\opencv\build\etc\lbpcascades`:

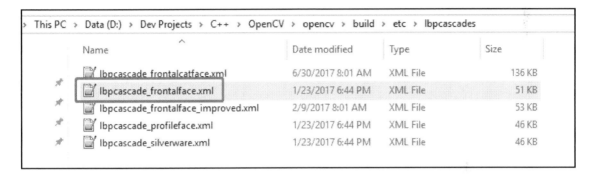

You want to copy `lbpcascade_frontalface.xml` into the scripts folder in Unity. (My project has everything in an XML folder, as I have many more `.xml` files to play with.)

Finally, we just need to create a plane to face the camera.

The last step is to attach the `OpenCVFaceDetection` script to the plane.

Now, the project will compile and run appropriately (if you get a dll import error, make sure you have the dll set to **x86-x64** and that the project is built for **Windows**):

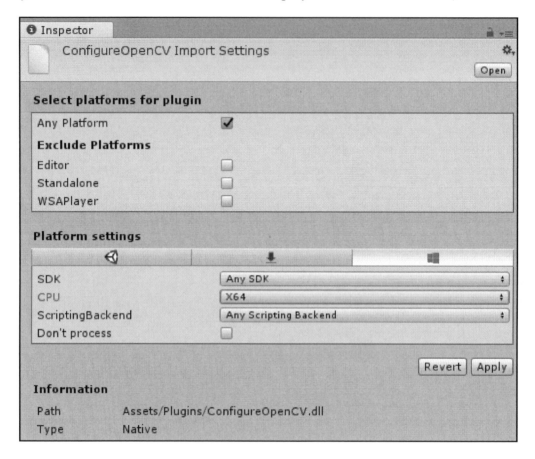

Summary

In this chapter, we learned how to use CMake to build OpenCV from source, to import it into Unity, and create an AR application similar to many on the market that are able to add images over a person's face and track their movements reliably, by using OpenCV and DLib FaceLandmark Detector, using Dlib C++Library.

In the next, and final, chapter, we will look into building for MR devices such as HoloLens. As a short teaser, MR incorporates elements from AR and VR into a single game or application, which can prove to have massive and interesting effects.

Questions

1. OpenCV is cross-platform and can work with Android, Linux, MacOS, iOS, Windows, HoloLens, and Oculus Rift:

    A.) True
    B.) False

2. The Dlib C++ Library is required to make OpenCV work on Windows:

    A.) True
    B.) False

3. OpenCV cannot be built from source:

    A.) True
    B.) False

4. Unity is not compatible with OpenCV:

    A.) True
    B.) False

5. You can use OpenCV with ARKit, ARCore, and Vuforia:

    A.) True
    B.) False

6. OpenCV is a library designed for machine learning and computer vision:

    A.) True
    B.) False

7. OpenCV can be used with AR, VR, and MR project types:

    A.) True
    B.) False

Further reading

- For the free assets that give you deeper insight into how to use OpenCV with Unity, you can download them from this GitHub link: `https://github.com/EnoxSoftware/OpenCVForUnity`
- To read the documentation on the Dlib C++ library, go to `http://dlib.net/`.
- To learn about the methods, properties, fields, and OpenCV tutorials in C++, Python, and Javascript, and to gain deeper understanding of how OpenCV is put together, you can go to this link: `https://docs.opencv.org/3.4.1/`

To the HoloLens and Beyond

8

In this chapter, we will look into how we can work with HoloLens to understand how to make **Mixed Reality** games and apps. The main focus will be to code with the HoloLens device in mind but be able to use the simulator for both the HoloLens and the Mixed Reality viewer. This will allow us to be able to test and view what is happening, regardless of whether we have the actual HoloLens device.

The learning objectives of this chapter are as follows:

- Learning what Mixed Reality is
- Understanding how Mixed Reality works
- Implementing a basic Mixed Reality prototype

What is Mixed Reality, and how does it work?

Mixed Reality is known as **MR** or **XR** (**extended reality**) and can refer to Augmented Reality, Virtual Reality, a combination of AR and VR into a single application or game, or it can be a reference to the game world being driven and modified by the real world. There are many ways to incorporate aspects of both **Augmented Reality** (**AR**) and **Virtual Reality** (**VR**) and by extension XR into a single application or a game.

It should be noted that Microsoft exclusively uses the MR for Mixed Reality; however, the terms XR and MR can be used interchangeably, with people being able to understand what you are referencing.

Let's take a look of a few notable examples of Mixed Reality games by Gbanga Millform Inc and dissect why they are Mixed Reality instead of just AR or VR games. Two games that I feel are very notable are Smart Urban Golf (`https://gbanga.com/gameography/smart-urban-golf/`) and Urban Hunt (`https://gbanga.com/gameography/gross-stadt-jagd/`).

Urban Hunt

Urban Hunt is an iOS and Android platform real-time game where players have to run and escape from a car that is hunting them throughout the city of Zurich. The game lasts anywhere from 90 minutes (one-and-a-half hours) to 150 minutes (two-and-a-half hours). The winner receives a Mercedes-Benz CLA Shooting Brake car in real life. Look at this screenshot:

The text in this image is not important. It's an image of Urban Hunt in use

The game incorporates GPS and location-based data to build the game world. The game is built to be played by everyone in the city of Zurich. The game has an AI that you the player have to run away from in real time.

Now, let's break down what is AR, VR, and MR about this game.

Right away, we can see that there are no elements of VR added to this game at all. So, we don't have to worry about that aspect of MR. It utilizes GPS, location data, and the city map of Zurich in the game. This means the game has some aspects of AR built into it by design. Moving on, it has MMO elements; this is neither AR or VR specific, but rather just massively multiplayer-online-game specific. Finally, the AI is what you the player have to run away from. This is where XR or MR comes into play. The reason for this is you don't control the character with button prompts; you are the character, and it is based on your real-life walking and running movements. This is the aspect of augmenting the game world with real-world interactions or, conversely, augmenting the real world with a game world.

Now, you might be thinking, *that last sentence is the literal definition of AR*, but let's break it down further. The game is not projecting into the real world, nor is the real world being fully projected into the game. The AI solely lives in the game world and you (the player) are simultaneously in the game world and the real world. You still have to pay full attention to the rules and the AI of the game world, in addition to the rules and struggles of real life. This is how it is Mixed Reality, instead of just Augmented Reality.

Smart Urban Golf

Smart Urban Golf is a game where you play golf using your cell phone as the club, and you hit golf balls in the game world. You can practice by playing the driving-range mode, which makes the game generate random courses based on your current position, or you can play in a live tournament mode where you compete with others for the highest score on the online leaderboards.

Look at this screenshot:

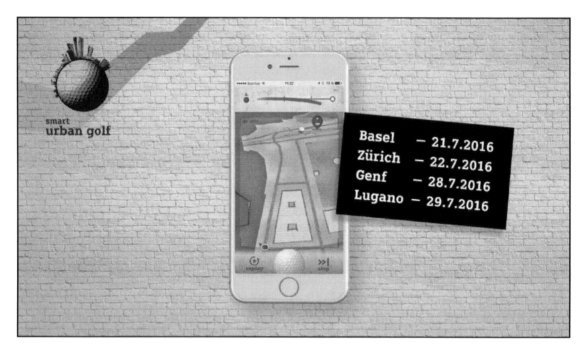

Smart Urban Golf

Breaking down the elements of the game, we can see that the golf club being the phone automatically places AR as one of the technologies being utilized. The location-based random courses means that Geolocation and GPS are being heavily utilized, which is mainly found in AR applications. Competing with others is a standard game mechanics. The ball is living in the game world only but is affected by the golf club (your cell phone), so the game is XR or MR.

XR applications in media

With these two example games being showcased, we should have a better idea of what XR or MR is. But I think we can go a bit further—what about using VR and AR together? There are certain people on YouTube who utilize the mixture of AR and VR together so the viewer can see what they see in the game as well as their body positions at the same time as using VR applications. Take a look at this:

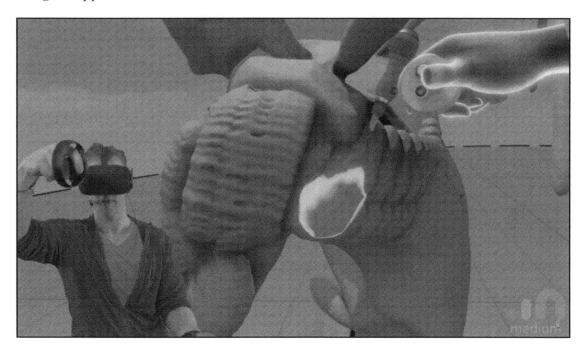

Jazza

Here we see Jazza from Draw with Jazza is sculpting a model in a VR application with Oculus Rift. We can see what he is sculpting along with him working from outside the application. This is an example of utilizing XR to enhance the viewing experience of a third party.

But let's also take a look at an XR video for gaming as well. Take a look at this:

Brometheus

Brometheus is playing a game called Nevrosa Prelude with the HTC Vive, and it is also a VR game but has AR projected to enhance the viewing experience of a third party.

XR with HoloLens

This is all well and good, but let's take one more look with a HoloLens example this time around. Take a look at this:

Minecraft

During the E3 demo of the HoloLens and Minecraft in 2015, we saw an AR projection of the game in the real world along with the person using the HoloLens in VR mode.

One last example with the HoloLens and **Windows Mixed Reality (WMR)** should suffice, as I think all of these examples combined into one really exemplify the MR or XR full experience. Let's take a look at this:

The text in this image is not important. It gives you an example of Mixed Reality with fragments

The game in this screenshot is called *Fragments*, which is an adventure-style detective game. What makes this MR or XR over pure VR is that the game will scan where you are and allow the objects and characters in the game interact with it seamlessly. As you can see from the screenshot, the character is sitting on the player's sofa.

What we have learned in this section is that XR or MR is essentially taking VR and AR elements and incorporating them into real-world environments and situations with seamless integration. This is the backbone of how we can take AR or VR to the next level for a proper Mixed Reality integration.

Getting Mixed Reality ready

The HoloLens requires your computer to meet a couple of requirements; this includes the requirements for supporting Hyper-V and being VR-ready. This is also true for utilizing the HoloLens emulator. So, what requirements do we need to meet? Take a look at the following:

- 64-bit Windows 10 Pro, Enterprise or Education editions.

 If you are using Windows 10 Home edition, it does not support Hyper-V or the HoloLens emulator.

- 64-bit CPU
- CPU with four or more cores, or multiple CPUs with a minimum total of four cores
- 8 GB of RAM or more
- GPU with support for DirectX 11.0 or later
- GPU with **WDDM (Windows Display Driver Model)**, 1.2 driver or later

We also need a bios that supports the following features, and have them enabled:

- Hardware-assisted virtualization
- **Second-Level Address Translation (SLAT)**
- **Hardware-Based Data Execution Prevention (DEP)**

Microsoft has a handy list of specifications to meet, for both laptop and desktop computers, for minimum and recommended settings. Alternatively, you can use software on the Microsoft Store to run a PC check for compatibility (`https://www.microsoft.com/en-us/p/windows-mixed-reality-pc-check/9nzvl19n7cnc`).

	Minimum	Recommended
Processor	**Notebook:** Intel Mobile Core i5 7th generation CPU, Dual-Core with Hyper Threading **Desktop:** Intel Desktop i5 6th generation CPU, Dual-Core with Hyper Threading **OR** AMD FX4350 4.2Ghz Quad-Core equivalent	**Desktop:** Intel Desktop i7 6th generation (6 Core) **OR** AMD Ryzen 5 1600 (6 Core, 12 threads)
GPU	**Notebook:** NVIDIA GTX 965M, AMD RX 460M (2GB) equivalent or greater DX12 capable GPU **Desktop:** NVIDIA GTX 960/1050, AMD Radeon RX 460 (2GB) equivalent or greater DX12 capable GPU	**Desktop:** NVIDIA GTX 980/1060, AMD Radeon RX 480 (2GB) equivalent or greater DX12 capable GPU
GPU driver WDDM version	WDDM 2.2 driver	
Thermal Design Power	15W or greater	
Graphics display ports	1x available graphics display port for headset (HDMI 1.4 or DisplayPort 1.2 for 60Hz headsets, HDMI 2.0 or DisplayPort 1.2 for 90Hz headsets)	
Display resolution	Resolution: SVGA (800x600) or greater Bit depth: 32 bits of color per pixel	
Memory	8 GB of RAM or greater	16 GB of RAM or greater
Storage	>10 GB additional free space	
USB Ports	1x available USB port for headset (USB 3.0 Type-A) **Note: USB must supply a minimum of 900mA**	
Bluetooth	Bluetooth 4.0 (for accessory connectivity)	

Microsoft specs

Hyper-V must be enabled on your system. Let's follow these steps:

1. To enable Hyper-V, go to the **Control Panel**:

2. Select **Programs**:

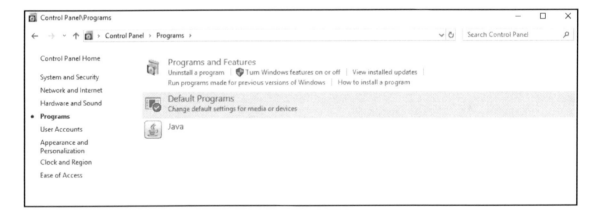

3. Select **Programs and Features**:

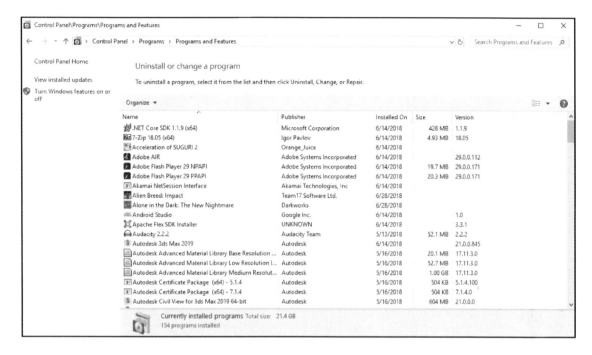

4. Select **Turn Windows features on or off**:

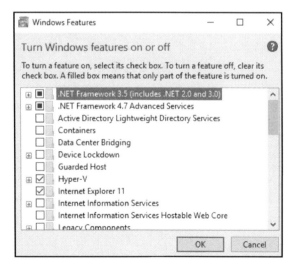

Windows features

5. Select all Hyper-V features by putting a check mark in and clicking the **OK** button:

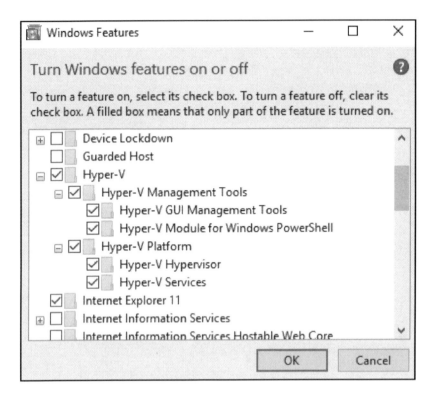

Enable Hyper-V

Next up, we need to be absolutely certain that we have Visual Studio set up in the proper manner. Follow these steps:

1. Open Visual Studio Installer from your Start menu. If you have the Visual Studio Community edition, it will work too:

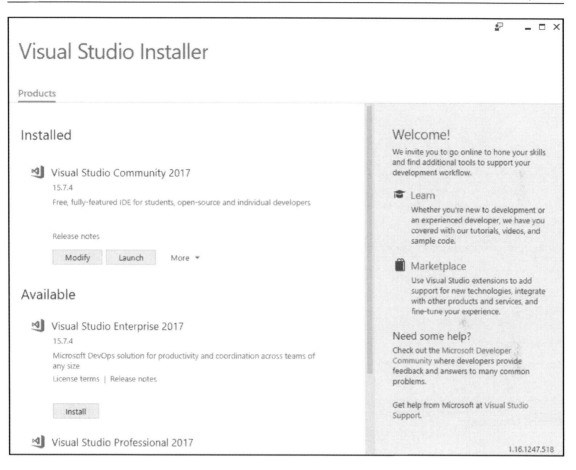

VS Installer

 We need to make certain that we have the most up-to-date version of Visual Studio. So, if it tells you to update instead of modify, do the update first.

2. Now we need to click on **Modify** and, then, once things are ready, click on **Individual components**:

Workloads	Individual components	Language packs	Installation locations

Modifying — Visual Studio Community 2017 — 15.7.4

Individual components

3. Scroll down until you see the list of Windows 10 SDKs. We need the latest one, which is 10.0.17134.0, and also the Windows 10 SDK for UWP C#, which is version 10.0.16299.0:

Windows 10 SDK

4. The last thing we need to do, if you haven't followed any other chapter in this book, is to make sure your minimum version of Unity is 2017, although we will be using the latest version of Unity, which is 2018.1.6f1. If you don't have it, make sure to update using the Unity Hub:

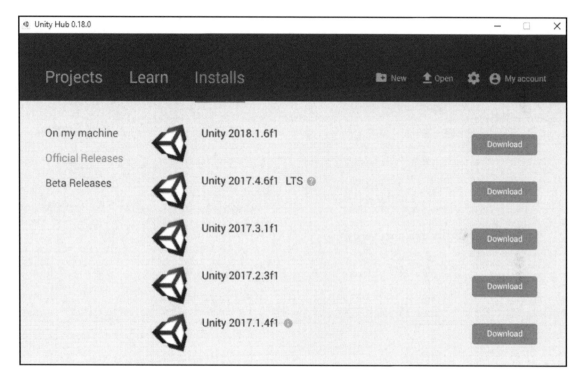

Latest Version of Unity

5. We also need to make sure we have the **Windows Store .NET Scripting Backend**, **Windows Store IL2CPP Scripting Backend**, and **Windows IL2CPP Scripting Backend**, to make sure we can translate from Unity specific code over to Windows code effectively:

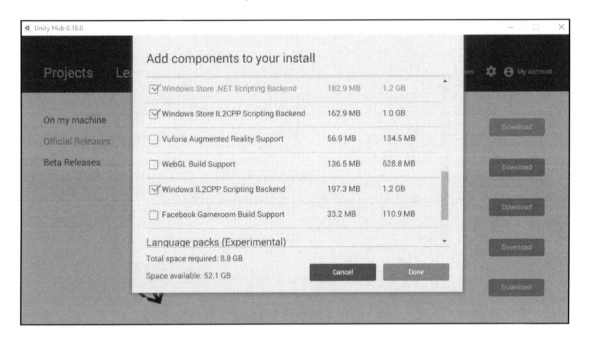

Unity Components

It will require a total of 8.8 GB in size on your hard disk.

Project overview

This project will be a basic prototype that will make sure that we can simulate a basic model can be displayed when viewed in HoloLens.

Playing with Mixed Reality

Let's begin by first downloading the model we will be using with this project. Once again, let's follow these steps:

1. Go to `turbosquid.com` and type `scifi` as the search parameters:

2. Next, change the pricing to **Free**:

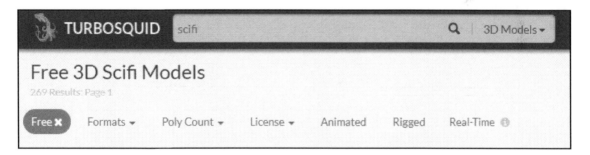

3. Find one you like. I like robots and I use FBX format, as I find it easy to use with multiple projects and game engines. So, I will select this one:

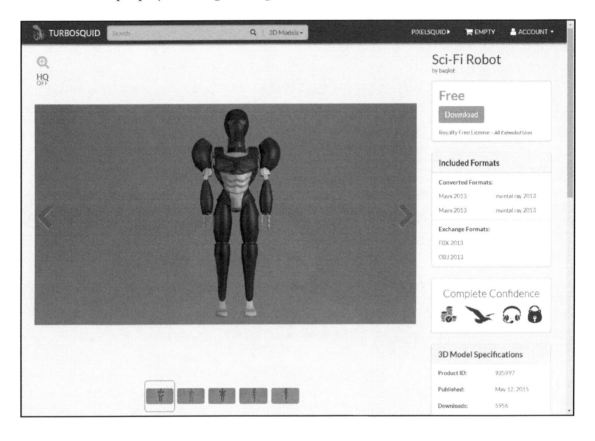

4. It will take you to a download page, so make sure you select the correct file you want and if it has a `textures` folder, download that as well:

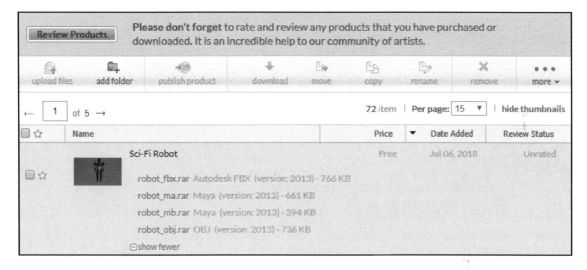

Download robot

5. Go to the folder where you downloaded the zip file and extract it:

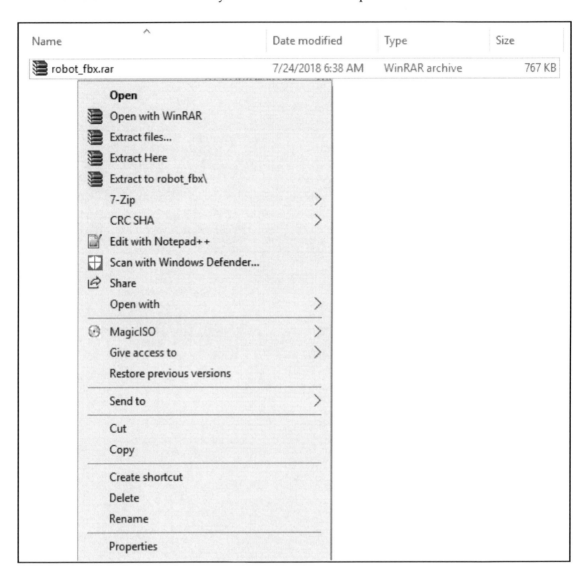

6. Now we can jump into Unity. Create a new project and I will call this one `Chapter8`:

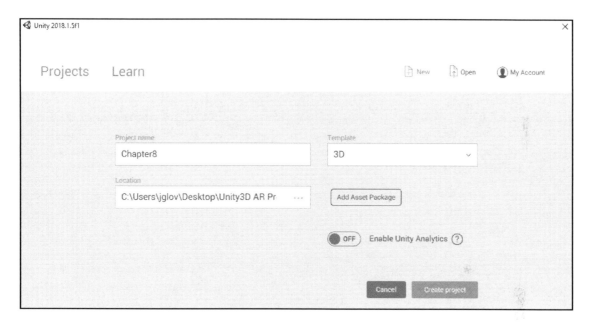

7. Create a new folder called `Models`:

8. Import the model into the project:

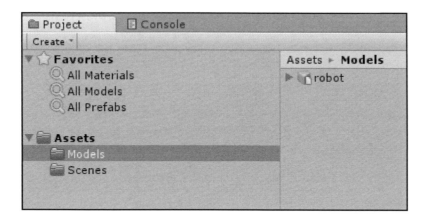

We now need to go through the steps to install the HoloLens Emulator. I should note that this will only work for Visual Studio, 2015 edition. If you have Visual Studio 2017 or later, you can use the Mixed Reality simulator that is built into the Windows 10 SDK. Let's follow the steps:

1. Go to `http://go.microsoft.com/fwlink/?LinkID=823018` to download the simulator.

2. Click on the installer to begin the installation process:

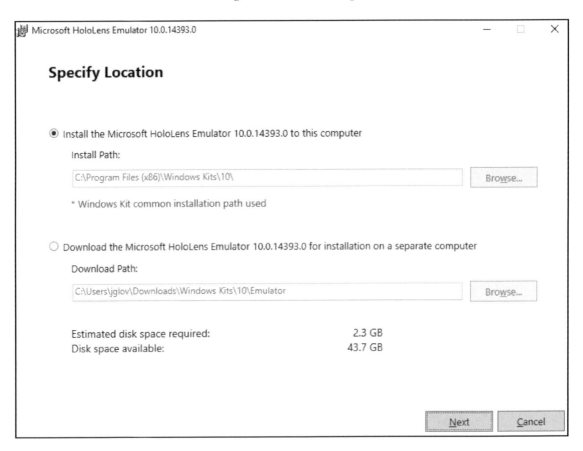

3. It will ask you if you want agree to using the CEIP program; choose your answer and click **Next**:

4. Next up will be the standard **Microsoft License Agreement**; I would suggest reading it to know what you are agreeing to, and then click **Accept** afterward:

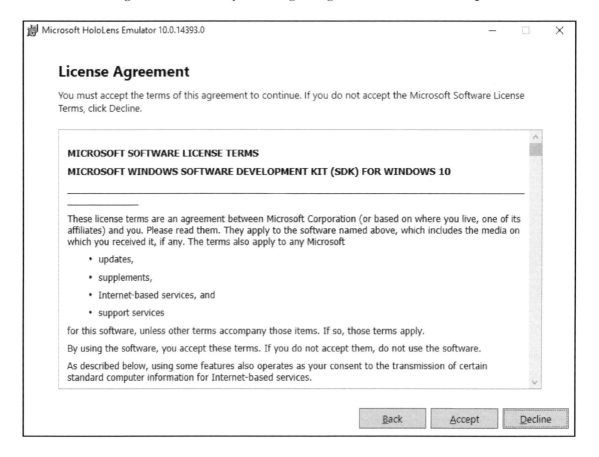

5. Select the features you want to install; I would suggest getting both the emulator and the templates for future reference. Click **Install**:

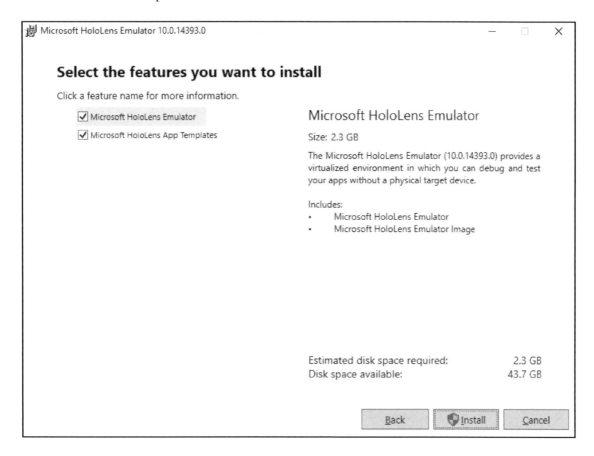

Now we can begin to set up the remaining portions of the project.

Setting up the camera

Since we or the user are using the HoloLens, we will be the first-person camera; it is important to remember that our starting position should always default to the Vector 3 values of x being 0, y being 0, and z being 0. Everything else should always be offset according to that knowledge.

1. So, the first thing to do will be to click on the camera in the **Hierarchy** pane:

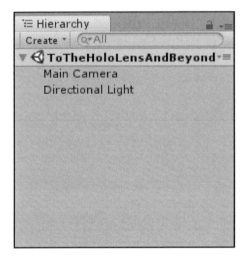

Camera selected

2. The default values for the camera are set to **X** being 0, **Y** being 1, and **Z** being
   −10:

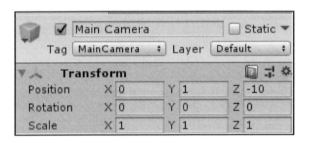

Default camera values

3. We need to change this to **X** being 0, **Y** being 0, and **Z** being 0. Look at this screenshot:

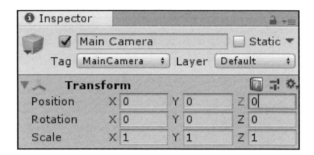

Modified camera values

4. With this being made for HoloLens, we don't need a Skybox texture; we want everything the camera renders. To do this, we need to change the **Clear Flags** from the default values.

5. The default values for the **Clear Flags** is **Skybox**:

Default Clear Flags

6. We are going to change it to **Solid Color**:

Clear Flags modified

7. Next, we need to click on the background option underneath **Clear Flags**, which will open a color-picker window and change the RGBA values set to this: 0,0,0,0:

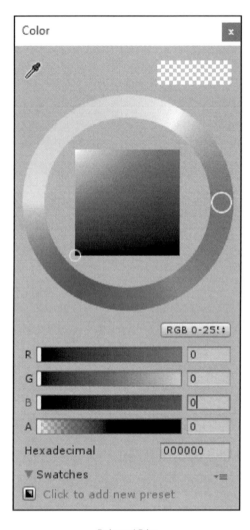

Background Color

If you are going for Mixed Reality applications targeted to immersive headsets, you can keep the default settings that the Unity camera provides for the **Skybox** being used.

Performance and quality control

As with any other game or application, performance is a very important thing to keep in mind. We need to maintain a high frame rate for Mixed Reality headsets and the HoloLens. As these headsets don't have many years of being on the market and aren't upgradable like PCs, Android phones, iOS devices, or consoles yet, it is best to keep the Quality Settings set to the lowest values possible.

1. To do this, click on **Edit** and look for **Project Settings**:

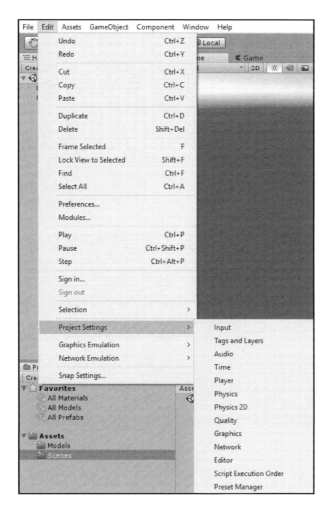

Project Settings

2. Click on **QualitySettings**:

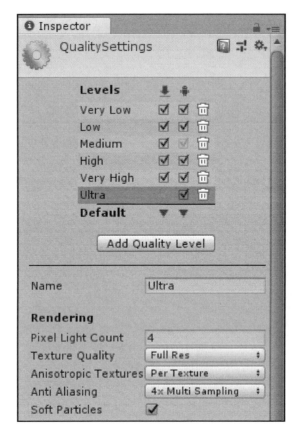

QualitySettings Defaults

3. Change the **QualitySettings** from **Ultra** or whatever your default values are to **Very Low:**

QualitySettings

4. The last thing to do is click on the arrows next to **QualitySettings** and set those defaults to be **Very Low** as well. Look at this screenshot:

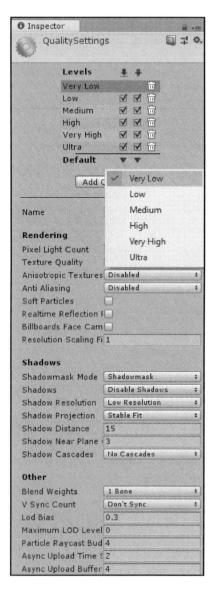

Set QualitySettings

Targeting the Windows 10 SDK

The next step is to make sure we set the target we need for building, in this case, the Windows 10 SDK. First things first, we need to change the scripting backend. Let's follow these steps:

1. To do this, open the **Build Settings** menu:

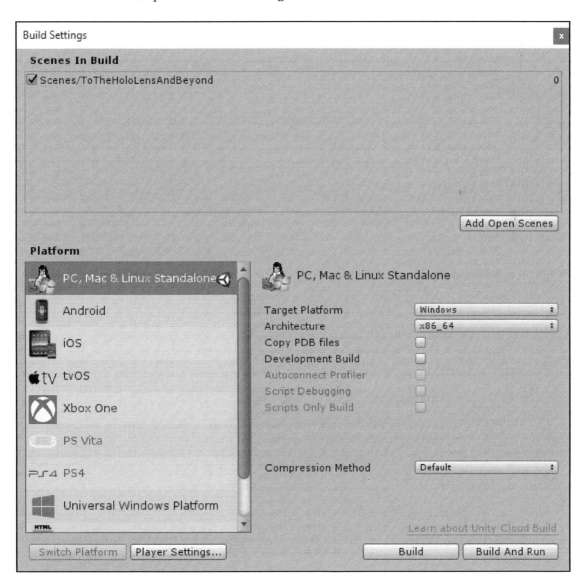

2. Now change the target from **PC, Mac & Linux** to **Universal Windows Platform**:

3. Click on **Player Settings** and look for **Configurations**. Your **Scripting Runtime Version** should be set to **.NET 4.x Equivalent**, **Scripting Backend** should be set to **.NET**, and **API Compatibility Level** should be set to **.NET 4.x**:

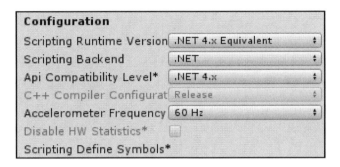

4. Now scroll down and select **XR Settings**:

5. Click on the box to put a check mark into the **Virtual Reality Supported** box to enable it; **Windows Mixed Reality** should automatically be there with **Stereo Rendering Method** defaulting to **Multi Pass**:

Do the robot

We are getting down to the final steps of this prototype project. So, let's add and configure our robot into the scene to get going into the home stretch. You know what to do—follow these steps:

1. We need to add the **robot** to the scene:

Add robot

2. There are a few values we need to change, the first of which will be the position from the **Inspector** pane, then the rotation, and finally the scale. The default values place it to be at the origin of the player and is too big to be of any use currently:

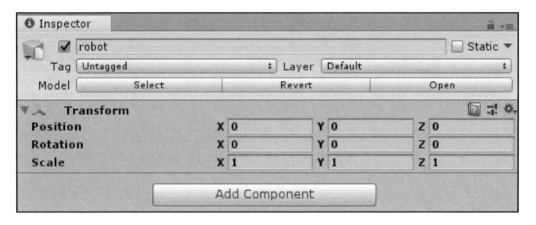

Robot Inspector

3. The **X** position should be set to 0.26, to account for the slight offset that we have from the groupings. The **Y** position should be set to 0, and the **Z** position should be set to 2:

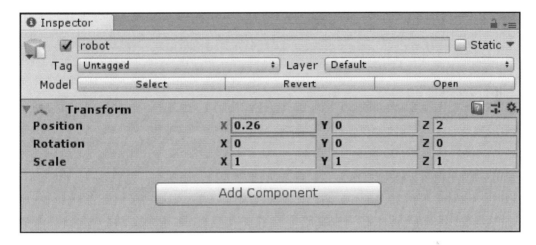

Position

4. Next up is the rotation; we will set the **X** rotation to be 45, the **Y** rotation to be 45, and the **Z** rotation to be 45:

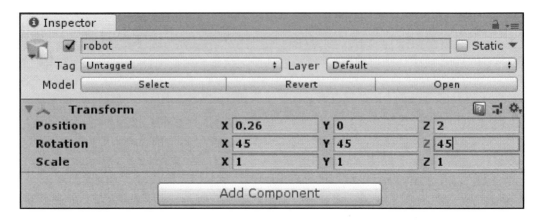

rotation

5. Last, but certainly not least, is the scale. The **X** scale will be set to 0.6, the **Y** scale set to be 0.6, and the **Z** scale to be 0.6:

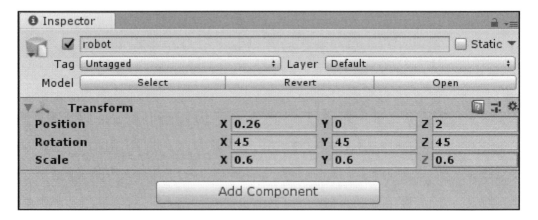

scale

Now we are ready to build and finish this off.

Building and deploying from Visual Studio

OK, this is the last bit, so follow these final steps:

1. Click on **Build Settings** in Unity:

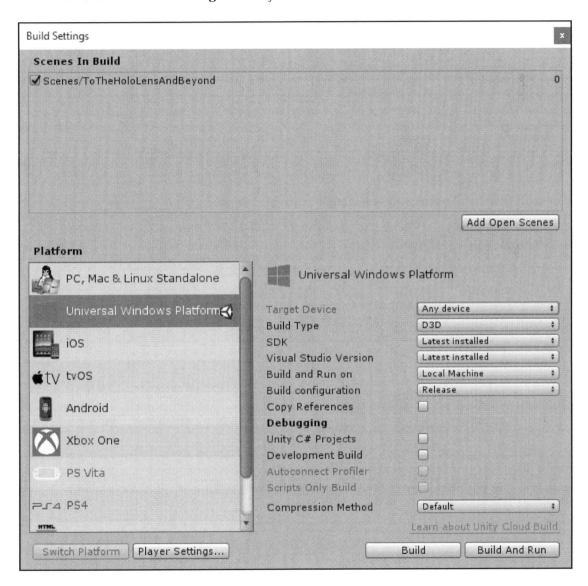

Build Settings

2. Make sure that **Unity C# Projects** has a check mark in it; everything else should have everything pre-setup appropriately:

Configuration

3. Click on **Build**:

Build

4. It will ask you for the folder you want to build to; create a new folder called App, and select it:

create folder

5. It will take a quite a few minutes to finish building, so be prepared for a wait:

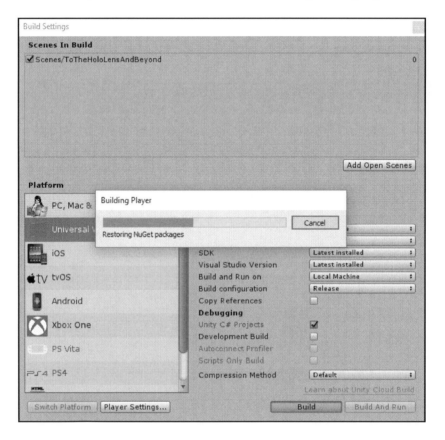

Building

6. Once complete, the folder should auto open; select the `App` folder, to have a look at it:

Name	Date modified	Type	Size
Chapter8	7/6/2018 7:02 PM	File folder	
Unity	7/6/2018 7:02 PM	File folder	
Chapter8.sln	7/6/2018 7:02 PM	Microsoft Visual S...	3 KB
UnityCommon.props	7/6/2018 7:02 PM	Project Property File	1 KB
UnityOverwrite.txt	7/6/2018 7:02 PM	Text Document	2 KB

App Folder

7. Click on the `Chapter8.sln` file to open it in Visual Studio:

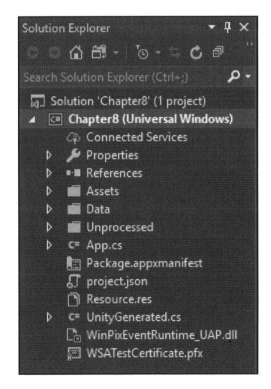

Visual Studio

8. Change from **Debug** to **Release**:

Debug

9. Change from **ARM** architecture to **x64**:

64 bit

10. Change from **Device** to the **HoloLens Emulator**:

HoloLens

11. Click on **Debug**, and **Start without Debugging**:

No Debugging

It will display in the simulator now. You have made your first prototype of a Mixed Reality program.

Summary

We learned about how Mixed Reality works and a few different techniques we can apply from the theory to practical use. We looked at some examples of Mixed Reality and set up our computers to build for Mixed Reality, using the HoloLens Simulator.

Moving beyond this book, I would suggest going more into the VR side of things or perhaps looking into what Microsoft has done for the HoloLens, as most of its applications and games are open source and on GitHub. There are many fascinating things to learn and incorporate into AR and XR applications; it is still a brand-new aspect of game and application development, so experiment and test out new ideas.

Questions

1. HoloLens requires Windows 8 SDK:

   A.) True
   B.) False

2. Mixed Reality is separate from VR and AR.

   A.) True
   B.) False

3. Unity can be set to regular PC building to build for Mixed Reality.

   A.) True
   B.) False

4. Installing HoloLens Simulator can be done via the Unity Editor.

   A.) True
   B.) False

5. HoloLens requires Windows 10 SDK.

   A.) True
   B.) False

6. Mixed Reality is only possible on iOS.

   A.) True
   B.) False

7. Augmented Reality extends the real world to the digital world.

   A.) True
   B.) False

8. Android Devices are AR devices.

   A.) True
   B.) False

9. HoloLens requires ARKit to run.

   A.) True
   B.) False

Further reading

- Microsoft has a fantastic collection of projects for you to go through that allow for you to build Mixed Reality projects. Check out this link: `https://docs.microsoft.com/en-us/windows/mixed-reality/holograms-101e`.
- Microsoft also has a walk-through on how to go about installing the tools and SDKs you need for building directly in Visual Studio. Check out this link: `https://docs.microsoft.com/en-us/windows/mixed-reality/install-the-tools`.

Other Books You May Enjoy

If you enjoyed this book, you may be interested in these other books by Packt:

Unity Virtual Reality Projects - Second Edition
Jonathan Linowes

ISBN: 9781788478809

- Create 3D scenes with Unity and other 3D tools while learning about world space and scale
- Build and run VR applications for specific headsets, including Oculus, Vive, and Daydream
- Interact with virtual objects using eye gaze, hand controllers, and user input events
- Move around your VR scenes using locomotion and teleportation
- Implement an audio fireball game using physics and particle systems
- Implement an art gallery tour with teleportation and data info
- Design and build a VR storytelling animation with a soundtrack and timelines
- Create social VR experiences with Unity networking

Getting Started with Unity 2018 - Third Edition
Dr. Edward Lavieri

ISBN: 9781788830102

- Set up your Unity development environment and navigate its tools
- Import and use custom assets and asset packages to add characters to your game
- Build a 3D game world with a custom terrain, water, sky, mountains, and trees
- Animate game characters, using animation controllers, and scripting
- Apply audio and particle effects to the game
- Create intuitive game menus and interface elements
- Customize your game with sound effects, shadows, lighting effects, and rendering options
- Debug code and provide smooth error handling

Leave a review - let other readers know what you think

Please share your thoughts on this book with others by leaving a review on the site that you bought it from. If you purchased the book from Amazon, please leave us an honest review on this book's Amazon page. This is vital so that other potential readers can see and use your unbiased opinion to make purchasing decisions, we can understand what our customers think about our products, and our authors can see your feedback on the title that they have worked with Packt to create. It will only take a few minutes of your time, but is valuable to other potential customers, our authors, and Packt. Thank you!

Index

Printed in Great Britain
by Amazon